Victim No More

Also by Jean Carlton
Panic No More: Your Guide to Overcome Panic Attacks

To order books, write or call: Stonehorse Press, P.O. Box 701595, Tulsa, OK 74170 (918 488-9530). Order form on page 288.

Victim No More

Jean Carlton

STONEHORSE PRESS
Tulsa, Oklahoma

Stonehorse Press
P.O. Box 701595
Tulsa, Oklahoma 74170

Cover Design by Dennis Teutschel

First Stonehorse Press Printing June, 1995
10 9 8 7 6 5 4 3 2 1

Library of Congress Catalog Card Number: LC # 94-69286
ISBN# 0-9639632-7-9

Printed in the United States of America

*To the loving
memory of my Mother*

Contents

Acknowledgments

The thanks and gratitude I express here can never be enough to my friends who helped me by giving countless hours making suggestions and proofing the manuscript. I am especially thankful to Jan Alan and Barbara Bartocci for their kind, loving, support and expert editorial abilities, along with just plain good company. Special thanks goes to Jeanie Lovelady and Deb Stone who gave me professional advice, too, critiqued the manuscript, and more good company.

Thank you, Janet Rains, for extending me hospitality and proofing the manuscript, along with your positive uplifting spirit and attitude. Thanks again, Mary Atwood, for going with me to conferences and conventions, and helping me bounce off ideas and concepts with you. You are a dear, long time friend. Veronica Winkler, words cannot come close to the admiration and respect I have for you. I thank you for your advice, guidance and proofing the manuscript.

Thanks goes to Carol Beem for proofing the manuscript and the many ideas she passed along my way. Sarah Allison is also due recognition for befriending me when I moved to Tulsa several years ago. She unselfishly gave me encouragement as a writer, and helped to promote my first book, *Panic No More*. Sarah acquainted me to many of the concepts involving women's issues

ACKNOWLEDGMENTS

which can be found woven throughout this book, and introduced me to other Tulsa leaders who have worked long and hard for women's rights. One such person, Barbara Santee, gave me so many ideas and inspiration in her talk, that many of those ideas can be found in this book. I am also indebted to Mary Parker for her professional wisdom and insight, and sharing that with me for inclusion in this book.

Thank you, Phil Hyde, for sharing your expertise about anger management with me. Thanks also goes to Jerry Gilbert for sharing his many witty sayings about the plight of women; Vol Kimberling for teaching me more about Eastern medicine and philosophy; and Paul Sommer for extending me the generosity of his professional services so I could keep my smile intact while working on this endeavor.

A special thanks goes to my teachers, Joan Borysenko, Jerry Densow, LeRoy Zemke, John Bradshaw and Jean Houston. With all the expert advice and careful, loving attention that this book has had, I hope the readers will find it enlightening and receive the benefit from the many hours of research and labor that gave birth to it.

Introduction

As our society has become more violent towards women, I felt the need for a feminist viewpoint of this phenomenon. The roots of violence against women come from long ago. Only in recent history has the violence been addressed as something that is deviant.

It has been my opinion for some time, and it is probably not new with me, as I first heard of the notion from Virginia Satir: any prevailing emotion or behavior pattern that consists for the duration of three generations, becomes imprinted in the genetic structure of the being.

Women have been victimized and controlled in many different ways throughout history. Many women have become used to it and accept the predetermination of their worth as worth less and therefore easy to use and control in a patriarchal society.

Some women fight the genetic pull towards subservience constantly. It is for all these women that I have written this book, along with the immeasurable help of the many women who have gone before me to break the shackles of restrain and domination over their being.

It is time we all said enough, and mean it. It is time the laws protecting women were used for them instead of against them. It is time the men who abuse and kill women are given a clear message: They can no longer pay outrageous fees to lawyers to get them off murder charges for killing their spouses who choose to leave them and no longer live in fear.

All women have a right to live their life without fear. Women's rights are human rights—to go anywhere, anytime they choose without fear, the same as men. They have a right to dress and feel comfortable in their bodies without reproach from a society that attempts to dictate what the female sex is to look like. Men aren't put under these restraints. Neither should women.

Women have a right to the same earning power as men, the same promotional advantages, the same respect and status all their lives regardless of their age—with or without a marriage ring—viewed by many men as a symbol of property ownership.

It is time for women to take back control over their lives, their bodies, and the terms under which they choose to have relationships with men, instead of allowing themselves to be defined by them. *Victim No More* explores these aspects of women's reality, attempting to set forth some solutions for these old, old, problems.

Chapter One

Cultural Victimization

It is evident not only when you pick up the newspaper or watch the evening news, but through your own pain and sufferings that our culture is violent! What sustains the violence that permeates our society? Why is it getting worse? Why are women and children the most likely victims?

Violence is about power and control. This theme extends from child abuse to conflicts between nations. In American society, violence and abuse translate into the power to control those who are seen as weaker and vulnerable, mainly women and children. This ancient concept of the powerful ruling the weak is known as *might is right*. Ruling by force and manipulation is the basis of male dominance in our patriarchal society.

Over the centuries, the ways of domination have had many facets—force, coercion, manipulation, even burning witches at the stake—but the focus has always remained the same: the control and suppression of the weakest, often, but not always, women and children.

Domestic violence is an oxymoron because there is no way you can "domesticate" or "tame" violence. The term itself is a violation. Calling violence "domestic" simply because it is perpetrated by a mate or a relative, negates the terrible damages inflicted on women (and also many times on men as not all women are passive victims to brutality), and gives society, including the legal and judicial authorities, moral permission to treat it as less serious "violence."

The police will often ignore a brutal attack by a husband or lover, when any stranger who had stabbed, beaten or strangled the woman in the same way, would have been arrested and convicted. Violence in the home also takes the lives of men and children as women are now fighting back, and some men kill themselves after they kill their wife and children.

ELDER ABUSE

Violence within the family system is not confined to wives, lovers, or children. More often than we want to believe, it also includes neglect of, and violence against the elderly, seventy-five percent of whom are women. Older women, in particular, are victimized by their own irresponsible, cruel, disinterested or drug or alcohol addicted children and/or grandchildren who beat them, rob them and, in some instances, kill them.

Older citizens, particularly women, are victimized by scam artists, (religious and secular), who steal their life savings, and leave them destitute and penniless. They are victimized by nursing homes which tie them up, overdose them with mind-numbing drugs, and who physically abuse them and threaten to kick them out of the nursing home if they complain.

VIOLENCE AND WOMEN'S HEALTH

Violence within the family system is not the only kind of violence that impacts women's health and security in this country. Violence in the streets kills their children and men, and leaves women living in poverty, fear, and despair. Street violence strips all of us of peace of mind. Parents worry if their children will return from school unharmed, without being kidnapped or killed by some crazed lunatic. On the streets, we worry about our own personal safety. We do our best to protect ourselves from muggers, purse snatchers, car hijackers and rapists.

There is the violence of forcing women to have children against their wishes, by keeping birth control methods so expensive poor women cannot afford them; by instituting laws which erode the ability of poor and young women to legally and safely terminate an unwanted pregnancy; by intimidating and even killing abortion providers to discourage them from providing this much needed service to women.

There is the violence of men who know they are infected with HIV and yet deliberately pass the virus into their female partners in some sort of macabre "get even" justice. There is the violence of men who refuse to use condoms (the most effective protection against venereal diseases such as herpes, chlamydia, and gonorrhea), leaving women with infection, pain, sterility, and complications during pregnancy.

There is the violence of rape, incest and sexual harassment. It is estimated that there are a million unreported rapes each year in this country. Only about ten percent of rapes are reported. Of that ten percent, only a few rapists ever come to trial and are convicted. Many of the convicted receive relatively light sentences. The damage of rape can last a lifetime. Even after the initial trauma has abated, somatic and psychological symptoms may surface and disrupt and incapacitate the victim.

"Date rape" is another form of violence. Although a serious crime, it is often trivialized. "Date" implies a modicum of consent on the part of the female simply because she agreed to social activity. Rape is rape, regardless of the title affixed to it, and the fact that a woman agrees to see a man socially does not give him license to attack her.

The same is true of incest, a horrendous act perpetrated against both male and female children. Some babies as young as two months old have been found with gonorrhea of the mouth, and girls as young as eight years old have been impregnated by their fathers. One incest victim gave birth to three babies, before she was fifteen years old. All fathered by her father.

As a society, we are just beginning to see the pain, rage, shame, guilt, confusion, depression, repression, and self-hatred which results from having been victimized by incest. Like "date rape," this crime is also trivialized by definition. "Child molestation" is not molestation. It is the rape of a child—of a child's body, a child's mind, and a child's trust. Rape is more than penetration, because rape is violence, not sex. This is true regardless of how harmless the sexual aggression may appear.

Some critics argue that rape means that sexual penetration has occurred; and anything else is not so severe. Those critics do not understand the dynamics nor the lasting damage of incest and child molestation. And we now have detractors who claim that psychologists are planting "false memories" about incest in the minds of women and children. This is just another part of the backlash against women who are attempting to take control of their lives and their bodies.

Sexual harassment? You wouldn't define that as an act of violence? It certainly is an act of aggression. When it threatens a woman's livelihood (particularly if she is a single parent), it is an act of economic violence that places her under terrible stress in the workplace. Do we know how many sick days are taken simply to get away from her harasser for one day? Do we know how many stress related illnesses are caused by these untenable situations? How many women lose their health insurance coverage because they are fired or quit a job where they are being harassed?

It is not necessary to punch a woman in the face in order to damage her. What about the violence of men who have fathered children and yet refuse to pay child support, forcing many women into poverty and a good number of them onto welfare?

This economic trauma is not seen as "true" violence, but it is violence nonetheless. If women cannot afford health insurance, medical and dental care, medicines, therapy, or proper nutrition, for themselves or their children, their physical and economic status will be negatively impacted. Eventually their problems become your problem and my problem.

Violence impacts all of us. It reduces the moral fiber of our society. It also hurts our pocketbooks in multiple ways such as increased medical costs and higher taxes. We don't know how many women and their children have been deprived of health insurance coverage and pensions because of divorce.

There are many old sayings about men and women, their virtue, economic and social status. For instance: "Most women are one man away from poverty." "Women have a past, men have a future." "There's not a pot so crooked that there's not a lid to fit it." Some even warn about the plight of women and their relationship to men as they grow older:

"When you are young, all you need is a pleasant smile.
When you are twenty, all you need is a pretty face.
When you are thirty, all you need is a good figure.
When you are forty, all you need is a good personality.
When you are fifty, you just need ready cash in the bank."

The "Rule of Ten" applies to those who would be tempted to marry for security. "You can marry in ten minutes more than you can make in ten life times. But, you will work ten times harder for it."

The traditional marriage for security has now become its own nightmare. Almost half end in divorce. A recent study reports that incomes for men increase forty-three percent the year they divorce, and women's incomes decrease seventy-three percent. Each year, divorced women with children are the largest group entering the poverty cycle.

Many more younger women remarry (forty-eight percent in their twenties, thirty-three percent in their thirties, and eleven percent in their forties) and improve their financial status through successful remarriages or by new careers. The study reported that few divorced women in their fifties remarried (Wallerstein and Blakeslle 1989).

However, it has been my observation, that if an older woman wants to remarry, she can usually find a mate. Many women in their fifties and sixties simply choose not to remarry.

Although the government's refusal to fund affordable day care cannot be called an overt act of violence against women, it nonetheless springs from the same well. Each day, the lack of affordable, dependable, day care forces women, and increasingly men, to live lives filled with fear, uncertainty, psychological and financial stress. Any number of other pressures interfere with their ability to do their jobs well, to be good parents, and to have a reasonable quality of life for themselves and their children.

Parents not only worry about whether their children are learning constructive things in day care, but today they also worry that their child will be raped, beaten, shot or kidnapped by a day care worker with a history of mental illness or a criminal record.

Many young children go home from school and wait unattended for their parent(s) to return from work. They are influenced by the violence they watch on TV and their neighborhood friends joining gangs.

When we send our children to school, we never know if they will come home alive or if they will be stabbed, shot or physically beaten, or robbed by a fellow student. Will our teenager be killed if we let him or her work in a fast food restaurant?

Will terrorists bomb a building, as recently happened in Oklahoma City, killing and maiming our babies, husbands, sisters and brothers? Will our husbands come home from the office without being massacred by a disgruntled co-worker or a psychotic with a gun? Will we ourselves be kidnapped in the parking lot at Wal-Mart's or gunned down by an irate motorist who's seen Pulp Fiction or too many Stallone or Schwarzenegger movies?

Even when it doesn't batter a woman's body, violence profoundly impacts her life. Women are the foundation blocks of the family. When any member of her family is the victim of violence, so is she. When her children are maimed and hurt, so is she. When her husband is injured or killed, so is she. When her parents are abused and treated as less than human, so is she.

As a society, we claim to revere and respect women and children, yet we spend more money on violent sports than we do on programs to improve the lives of women and children. We claim to be a peace loving country, yet at no time in our history have we had such universally pervasive violence in our media, our schools, our homes, and our workplaces. We claim to be a God loving nation that respects life, yet the gutters run red from the slaughter in our streets.

What is at the root of this violence against women and children? It is in all kinds of homes—mansions as well as shacks, apartments as well as college dorms, farmhouses as well as rose-covered bungalows.

The root of this violence is the total lack of respect for another human being's uniqueness, autonomy, and value. Women are not valued, therefore they can be raped, beaten, tortured and killed. Children are not valued, therefore they can be neglected, abused and thrown away. Older people are not valued, therefore they can be ignored, abused, tormented and left to die unattended in their own urine. Blacks and Hispanics are not valued, therefore, they can kill each other and no one cares.

Until we stop the violence that has been perpetuated in every aspect of life, the violence against women and children will not stop, nor will violence anywhere else. Until little boys learn that little girls are just as valuable as they are, and that hitting and punching and kicking, are not the ways to settle disputes; until grown men stop glamorizing, packaging and selling violence, particularly against women, society's violence will not stop. Until alternatives to violence are considered as the first option and not the last one, until manhood is proven by mature judgment and understanding, not punching someone's lights out; until men understand that they are the only ones who can stop the male violence, this senseless slaughter will go on and on and on.

Violence against women does not stop at the door of their homes or even at the border of their countries. Violence against women is pandemic, universal and institutionalized. Witness the brutality of clitorectomies forced on young girls in African nations, or Brazilian laws which permit women to be murdered with immunity if they are suspected of cheating on their husbands, or the fact that over one million females are completely missing from the population of China due to infanticide of unwanted female babies.

Where, why, and how did the devaluing of women get started? What has perpetuated it? For these answers, a historical perspective is needed.

WITCHES

During the middle ages, nine million people were burned as witches; most of them women (Walker, 1988). Women were called witches if they had warts and skin growths. Many were healers and midwives. Midwives, the Catholic Church claimed, harmed the faith by easing women's pain in childbirth, imposed on women as punishment for Eve's original sin. Not only were midwives burned for witchcraft, the women who requested help for a difficult labor could be condemned also. Their children were sometimes burned and murdered.

Christianity provided men's primary rationale for taking the practice of healing away from women and converting it into a lucrative male-dominated profession using leeches and lancets instead of women's natural herbs. After that, women were barred from the universities and medical schools, and denied entrance to libraries, further robbing them of a means of self-support.

Church laws banned women from the following careers: healer, landowner, merchant, record keeper, spiritual advisor, prophet, funerary official, lawmaker, judge, historian, and craftswoman. Due to these restrictions, women became economically dependent upon men, who then viewed them as inferior and defective.

Some spiritual beliefs continue to blame women for their own abuses by prophesying that they deserved to be abused because they did the same thing to others in a past life. When women accept this guilt promoting tactic, they become stuck in their trauma, because they are denied access to their right to grieve, own their own anger and sadness, and recover their power.

Since manhood was defined as strength, courage, superior and intelligence, men had to project their weakness and inadequacies onto someone else. Women suited their purpose perfectly. They became the depositories for men's negative feelings and then blamed for everything that went wrong.

With females stripped of livelihoods, their survival depended upon marriage. Even so, if a woman exerted her independence, her husband could claim her a witch and have her tried and burned. In that climate, women learned to insure their well being by becoming passive, subservient, and people pleasing.

The Church went so far as to declare that the soul of the unborn child came from men's semen. The female womb was regarded only as "fertile soil" where the fetus awaited birth. A woman's mind was considered inferior and incapable of learning.

Through the centuries, many women came to view themselves with the same contempt men did. They began to believe the myths perpetrated about them by a patriarchal society. Examples of the myths are: "Men are smarter than women. Women are only good for: *preparing* meals, *having* children, and *cleaning* house."

INTERNATIONAL ATROCITIES

Many of these prejudices still influence women's lives. Look at the following examples of repression and violence against women to keep them in "their place." What is so frightening is that these things are going on around the world today. Can you imagine living in these circumstances and what it would do to you?

• In Switzerland, some counties still refuse women the vote. If a woman divorces, she is deemed incompetent to rear her own children and the court appoints a guardian to oversee her child's schooling and health care.

• An estimated eighty million women in Africa are sexually mutilated so their mates will not think them impure and reject them. In West Africa, Muslim girls with uncircumcised clitorises can't marry.

• Women are still sold into sexual and physical slavery in many countries around the world. After a house burned in Pakistan, the skeletons of four young women were found chained to beds in the basement.

• In Kuwait during the Iraqi war, the bodies of three young American girls were found. They had been missing for several years and had apparently been kidnapped from the United States and sold into sexual slavery in Kuwait.

• There were an estimated 5,500 dowry deaths in India last year. Young girls were burned to death in their sleep or otherwise dispatched, because the dowry paid by their families was not considered sufficient by the groom's family.

• Thousands of Muslim women must wear ugly and uncomfortable garb from head to foot or risk losing their lives. Two teenage Muslim girls were shot down in the streets in a middle-eastern country for not properly covering themselves. A teen Muslim girl in this country was stabbed by her father because she had "dishonored" him by getting a job at McDonalds.

• Thousands of Bosnian women were raped by Serb soldiers— a state sanctioned act.

It is important that women see the connection between the cumulative results of the cultural repression and what occurs as that repression escalates toward violence. The result is an attitude of *power and control*. Most cultures permit males of the world to treat women as important only as breeders, sexual objects, and household servants. The end result is to reduce women to interchangeable spare parts, and finally to expendable throwaways who can be abused, tortured, raped or killed depending upon the individual male's whim.

Women can break the chains of patriarchy and establish their own feminist (woman-centered) view of the world. Until then, we will live with male excesses of violence, and exploitation of other nations, the environment, animals, natural resources, and of course, women and children.

If this world is to be saved physically and spiritually, it will be the women who do it; and if we are interconnected and united, we can. After all, the womb is the most powerful force in the universe. That's why men try so desperately to control it.

THE BEAUTY QUEEN SYNDROME

Many strides have been made toward women's rights in the last two decades. Western women have gained legal and reproductive rights, may attend almost any university, enter any library, and compete in the job market along side men. They have overturned ancient and revered beliefs about their social role. But the American woman still earns $.70 to a man's $1.00.

As with children who are abused—and women have been abused for centuries—they will abuse themselves in the absence of an abuser. The results of centuries of suppression and denial of economic and political independence, have become generationally imprinted upon females, leaving them with culturally inborn traits of feelings of inferiority, passivity, people pleasing, and a basic lack of confidence, poor identity and economic understanding. Many women need courses in assertiveness training to help develop the confidence that centuries of undermining have destroyed.

In very subtle ways, society continues to reinforce the view of women as victims by encouraging them to think of themselves as contestants in a beauty queen contest. Nature abhors a vacuum, and when women started to liberate themselves, an onslaught of media manipulation took over to make women feel like failures and transfer the guilt. Women now mutilate themselves with tummy tucks, liposuction, facial peels, and breast implants to fit the images imposed on them by a male dominated fashion and beauty industry. When that's not enough, women continue to perfect themselves through anorexia, bulimia and compulsive exercise.

Once a woman's age shows on her face, she becomes invisible. People look straight through her as if she's not even there. Older women find it much more difficult to find employment, and when they do, much to their dismay, they may find their ability to command a livable wage has decreased, in comparison to younger women.

Older women find out that men their age date and marry women ten to twenty years younger. The TV news anchors, the older man - younger woman combination, resembles most men's second marriages. Where there is a power imbalance, the "Golden Rule" applies, "He who makes the gold also makes the rules."

Often, successful older men insist on an anti-nuptial contract when they remarry. So what a younger woman is actually getting in an older man, is someone she will end up taking care of, without benefit of a paycheck. If she should outlive her usefulness (age), she can be turned in for a younger model without much financial damage.

Our society says older men, despite lines in their faces and gray hair, look distinguished. Older women have far less status, or value, when they commit the unpardonable sin—aging. This double standard of value and worth equated with beauty and youth, robs and abuses women. It tells women they are only valued as objects, to be thrown away when youth is over.

Older women have valuable knowledge and experience, and it is exactly this that the patriarchal society wants to discredit. Many older women have found the confidence to eschew control. Younger women are urged to ignore their older counterparts, but by ignoring the knowledge and experience of their older "sisters," younger women symbolically cut themselves off at the knees. They lose the power, wisdom and continuity of identity with their female archetypes and mentors.

"You're never good enough, and you're certainly not OK the way you are," millions of women are told through a barrage of advertising from the cosmetic, diet, plastic surgery, and fashion industries. These billion dollar industries depend on undermining women's confidence and self-esteem in order to control them (tell them how to spend their money) and make enormous profits.

According to Naomi Wolf, author of *The Beauty Myth*, the average plastic surgeon makes $1,000,000.00 per year; that means, collectively, $300-million per year. The diet industry makes $33-billion; cosmetics, $20-billion; beauty pornography, $7-billion.

Enormous amounts of money are spent on advertising in

women's magazines, and on T.V.; everywhere you look, the faces and bodies of attractive young models promise—you, too, can look like a fashion model *if* you buy the products they are wearing.

These models get paid good money to look like they do. They diet, exercise and often have plastic surgery to enhance their looks. That's their business! By continually comparing yourself with these professional beauties you end up feeling like you are nothing but a bag of cellulite. Your confidence is shot, and you focus on what you can do to alter yourself accordingly, to relieve the guilt for being such an inadequate slob. Get the victim to blame the victim is the name of this game.

The beauty queen syndrome equates women's value with their bodies. The message is women are nothing without beauty. Sexual child abuse (one in three females are sexually abused in childhood) leaves a woman feeling inadequate, inferior, with a poor sense of self-worth and a shattered identity. She already has been given the message she is only good for the use of her body. The damaged goods syndrome makes women easy targets for revictimization. They will buy, do, be, whatever they can to feel acceptable. When the culture tells them they are not pretty enough, they fall for it.

Women obsessed with beauty may overspend on cosmetics, clothes, plastic surgery and dieting, and, yes, therapy—anything to make them feel better about themselves. The constant preoccupation with their appearance and not measuring up to the model ideal gives women ample reason to feel depressed. Instead of focusing on the real causes and working through the issues of their childhood abuse, many abuse themselves. Anorexia and bulimia kill. Constant dieting triggers those diseases.

The damaged goods syndrome that 100% of child abuse victims suffer, makes them never question that they are not good enough just the way they are. They will work harder, longer, suffer face lifts, face peels, liposuction, tummy tucks, breast implants, exercise to the point of exhaustion, diet, diet, diet, and then blame themselves when they age or have fat thighs.

It's a no win situation. It's as if women are in a beauty contest, and someone else is judging them—someone making profits. As long as the definition of "beauty" comes from outside women, they will continue to be manipulated by it.

In abusive homes the rules are arbitrary and can change at any time, and so do the rules of fashion that dictate what you *should* look like. If you follow their dictates, you are being used to meet someone else's needs and not your own. When you allow someone else to judge you, you are giving them your power. They are in control.

Chapter Two

The Victim Role

Even though women have been victimized by their families and society, labeling yourself a *victim* can trap you as surely as the abusive situations you have survived. Seeing yourself as having been victimized is a healthy part of recovery. Seeing yourself as a victim is not. It's like getting stuck in your own recovery process.

When you are betrayed and victimized in childhood, the bond of trust is broken. You feel utterly overwhelmed, helpless and powerless. You lose your identity. Because of the complete loss of control you experience, your crushed personality either disintegrates, fragments, or isolates and buries itself behind a wall so thick nothing can touch it again.

What is left of your psyche is like a burned out building, inhabited by memories and horrors. In the midst of this rubble, an elaborate, jumbled mass of defenses are developed to protect you. You acquire *learned helplessness* and numerous fears.

Childhood victimization teaches *learned helplessness*. You have been treated as if you are worthless, an object to be used and discarded, manipulated and violated. You probably feel as if a truck ran over you, backed up and did it again, but you hide those feelings, don't tell anyone about the horrors of the past, and try to act *as if* nothing happened. *Of course, you're normal!* You strive to put forth an appearance of perfect control, while inwardly your sides are shaking apart.

Bonita has three degrees and owns a successful business. She dresses right, looks right, appears self-assured and self-confident, but inwardly, she's scared to death. Bonita drinks every day. She questions her every move, her finances, if her husband loves her, or if he's seeing someone else. Since she married, she's been sick every day with some type of ailment. However, if you ask Bonita how she feels, she says, "Just fine."

This mask of defenses is designed to masquerade as sanity. This mask constantly surveys the environment and relationships and says, *what do you want from me? I'll give you what you want as quickly as possible to get it over with. I'll please you so you won't humiliate or embarrass me.*

You please others because you were trained through *learned helplessness* to think there were no other choices. You simply surrender what others want before things can be taken away. That's why you appear so generous. You do not know you can set boundaries and say, "No."

Problems represent further abuse, so you run from them. You haven't learned problem solving coping skills. You stuff feelings and deny your right to run your own life. You don't realize you take control of your life by what you allow to influence you.

A victim identity is a series of defenses that includes people pleasing, mind reading, catastrophizing, and panic attacks. No interior life is developed because the psyche is filled with terror and horror.

Feelings are numbed to avoid never ending fears. *What will the next abuse be? When will it happen?* All the psychic energy is exerted to defend or comply with attacks from the external world. Victims feel they have lost complete control over their lives.

Compounding this problem is the confusion all abused people seem to suffer. Since childhood abuse is seldom validated, victims are made to feel they "made it all up." Perpetrators count on their victim's confusion to conceal discovery of their criminal behavior. Remembrances of abuse are frequently repressed and buried, but the feelings from them continue to seep up from the deeps.

If you go to your doctor or family and tell how you feel, you are often told, "It's all in your head." You're handed a prescription, which further reinforces the idea, you made it all up.

AS IF BEHAVIOR

Abused people adapt by modeling what they consider appropriate behaviors and feelings. They develop the ability to appear *as if* everything is all right. They learn what feelings are

31

acceptable and act *as if* they are successful and doing all right. Unacceptable feelings, such as anger or sadness, are repressed.

Sensing their inner void and lack of identity, they are eager to attach a label to themselves. Any label or stereotype will do: alcoholic, sex addict, compulsive over-eater, victim, anorexic— the list could go on indefinitely. These labels describe how victims learn to cope with abuse.

Symptom identification happens in many twelve step recovery groups. People are always in the process of recovering. They never can really get on with life. They are asked to identify themselves by repeating "I'm an alcoholic" or "I'm a compulsive over-eater." When they identify with those phrases, "I'm a victim" or "I'm a mental patient" or "I'm an incest victim," they may stop the process of healing and get stuck in recovery.

This is not to say avoid twelve step programs, as they are enormously valuable and helpful to many people. But, do not get trapped into thinking that once you enter into a twelve step recovery program, your healing journey is over. It is just beginning, and it goes on beyond them. When you have mastered what they have to offer, *leave*, and get on with your life.

You may even identify with how you think someone else feels about you: "I'm bad, I'm a failure, I'm fat!, I'm broke, or I'm VVR (very, very rich)." You may constantly work harder and harder at your job to try and raise your low self-esteem. When your co-workers say, "You're such a hard worker!," you temporarily feel better about yourself.

As if type people easily become victims since a negative identity is better than no identity at all. This type of labeling leads into the same trap as victimization, because it is a one dimensional thinking of the self. At best, it's misleading; at worst, it entrenches a victim identity—and the denial of the self. Without access to your feelings, or the ability to trust them, you cannot learn from experience (because you don't trust your own perceptions). You fall for whatever people want from you, and may be revictimized again, and again, and again.

VICTIM IDENTITY

A victim identity puts the locus of control outside yourself onto the environment or other people. You try and adapt to outside events because you feel no active control within. It's called *learned helplessness*. You may compensate by assuming responsibility for others. The subconscious thinking behind this behavior is *other people can protect and take care of me if they're all right.*

For example, incest victims are selected by abusers who see them as emotionally vulnerable; usually the youngest or least experienced member of the family. Family members may have already started using the designated child as the family scapegoat to blame their problems, which further weakens him or her, and makes the child even more susceptible and needy for affection and attention.

In order to heal, you need a witness to your trauma, to affirm and validate it. Because childhood sexual abuse is often denied, you are made to feel it didn't really happen. Ironically, the denial of the trauma assures it will symbolically be repeated over and over.

The trauma continuously reenacts itself throughout life in the form of a repetition compulsion. You seek abusive or non-satisfying relationships where your needs are discounted. Physical symptoms may tell the story of what actually took place. "History repeats itself," Nietzsche wrote. That which is not remembered is doomed to repeat itself and tell the story of what actually happened through symptoms, abusive relationships, addictions and compulsions.

Abuse victims frequently mistake being cared about (loved) as being protected and taken care of (nurtured). Your sense of being protected may, in fact, be possessiveness and jealousy where you are held hostage. Abusers often present themselves as protectors, but what they are looking for is someone to control. If you don't take care of yourself, nobody else will. When you continue to look for protection from others, you put yourself in the victim trap.

Most often, the very person you think will save you, ends up being the one who revictimizes you in some way. Recognize this danger! The lesson to learn is that you have to take care of yourself. Do this by using the coping skills of assertiveness, limit setting and trusting your own healthy perceptions and feelings.

WHAT DOES IT MEAN TO BE A VICTIM?

Definitions and synonyms of victim abound: cheated, deceived; a person who suffers from a destructive or injurious action or agency; defrauded, hoodwinked, easy mark, scapegoat, lamb, patsy, sucker, fall guy; to exploit, maltreat, injure, persecute, oppress, enslave, wrong, brutalize, attack, martyrize, assault, fool, swindle, defraud, mislead, betray, delude, take in, trick, bamboozle, outwit, and double-cross.

Perhaps there are so many definitions and synonyms because there are so many, many ways to be victimized. Childhood abuse, because it makes you feel unworthy, insures there will be further abuses in adulthood.

Children can be victimized in multiple ways. One seemingly benign, but extremely destructive way, occurs when parents use a child to meet their own needs. The child is unloved for him or herself. The parents may use the child to be mother or father's best friend and confidant. Or the parents may dump unacceptable negative aspects of themselves on the child by saying, "you're selfish, nasty, and dumb."

The child may become the family scapegoat and be blamed for all the problems in the family. Then there is out and out emotional abuse, verbal battering, constant criticism, neglect, abandonment, physical abuse, sexual abuse, or simply not protecting the child from these dangers. Some children suffer from being ignored or never receiving focused attention. These abusive situations teach children that they are unworthy of respect, validation, and protection, and lead to further abuse during adulthood.

Children who are abused prior to age six may experience personality fragmentation. This disabling problem, commonly known as Multiple Personality Disorder, now renamed by the DSM IV (American Psychiatric Association: *Diagnostic and Statistical Manual of Mental Disorders*, Fourth Edition) as Dissociative Identity Disorder. Untreated child abuse can lead to a lifetime of depression, guilt, and low self-esteem—and continued revictimization.

Common types of revictimization include:
- Domestic violence—an oxymoron since violence is not domestic
- Choosing a relationship with a misogynistic (woman hater)
- Any form of rape—marital rape, date rape, or street rape; all share the same violence and abuse. Rape is rape.
- Sexual harassment—at work or in a relationship

Accepting the identity of a victim attracts disaster. *People who continue to see themselves as victims attract the conditions in life that affirm that kind of existence.* Saying you are a victim is like wearing a sign on your back that says, "Hit me, I'm a professional scapegoat. I can't control my own life or protect myself. Blame me for all your problems and inadequacies."

The word victim carries with it an energy of abuse. Although energy cannot be seen or heard, it's nevertheless there. Different energies operate on different frequencies and attract more of the same kind of energy. The energy of love attracts more love. The energy of victim attracts more victimization. Holding energy to attract more "like" energy is a technique of the masters. Be certain you are holding the kind of energy that is helpful and productive.

Dissolve negative energy once you have learned what it has to teach you. *Once a victim, twice a volunteer* is a warning to let the victim identity go. The energy of victim continues to be active and attract revictimization as long as there is repressed trauma. Doing discovery work is a major part of recovery. Protecting yourself during this process is very important. If you are not properly prepared for discovery, you can retraumatize yourself all over again.

You couldn't help what happened to you when you were little and powerless. And because you were abused, you may have grown up developmentally arrested. Now you may want, more than anything, to be protected by a powerful and loving person who will take care of you and give you everything you want. This overwhelming wish frequently results in idealizing the very person who harmed you in the first place. The problem with wanting your former caretaker to love and protect you is that it will never happen—you can never receive from others what you were cheated from in childhood.

You can spend the rest of your life being dependent on your parents or surrogate parents, (often disguised as therapists), and/or in abusive relationships. Hope overrides all your experiences; and you may think, "Someday I'll get the love I never received." All the while, you wonder why you never feel "good enough."

Learn to "take care of" and "care for" yourself. You can "reparent" yourself and learn to love and respect yourself and others. Someone else does not have to love or protect you for you to discover what love is. That's why all twelve step programs have a basic foundation in spiritual awakening. As you awaken spiritually, you will develop the ability to love, and receive love, and recognize the difference between love and abuse.

VICTIM NO MORE

Chapter Three

Discovering
Past
Abuse

When a child is sexually and/or physically victimized, the memories are usually repressed. It's too painful to remember. In fact, survival can depend on forgetting. Frequently, when children six or younger are abused, not only is the traumatic memory repressed, if there is no supportive person in the environment, the personality fragments. That's normal development for someone who has been traumatized.

When you are young, one traumatic incident can alter the course of brain development, and effect changes in brain chemistry for the rest of your life. Delayed, unresolved grief from childhood is the basis of Posttraumatic Stress Disorder. Tears have been found to have hormones in them that help normalize brain chemistry (John Bradshaw, The Core of Spirituality Lecture). Therefore, grieving the hurts of childhood is essential for the healing process.

Parents who are detached from their children, and/or abusive environments in which children grow up, can stimulate hyperarousal in children to the extent that they lose much of their ability to modulate anxiety and aggression. Parallels have been drawn between animal responses to inescapable shock and human responses to overwhelming trauma. In both, there is a depletion of catecholamines, and can result in psychological constriction and numbing (Kluft; Schetky,1990).

If you are uncertain if abuse occurred in your childhood, look over the list below and see how many of the listed symptoms you have.

Symptoms of childhood abuse include:
- absence of a *safe place*
- extreme or long lasting depressions
- inwardly seething with rage
- ulcers
- headaches, migraines
- *learned helplessness,* feeling you don't have any choices
- *learned hopefulness*
- taking a suggestion as a command
- suicide ideation and/or attempts
- alcoholism and drug addiction
- self-mutilation; cutting, hitting or burning oneself

- sliding or multiple personalities
- antisocial or extremely aggressive behavior
- excessive jealousy or possessiveness
- promiscuousness or prostitution
- extreme confusion and disorientation
- denial of past events
- sudden personality changes
- claustrophobia and all other phobias
- feeling trapped
- excessive fear or dislike of being touched
- fainting or hyperactivity
- repressed tears or screaming
- hearing voices in the head or body
- fearful clinging to childhood security
- outbursts of unreasonable violent rage
- passivity
- obesity
- compulsive overeating
- poor self-esteem
- anorexia
- bulimia
- feelings of hopelessness and despair
- feelings of self-contempt and self-loathing
- panic attacks
- epileptic seizures with or without organic evidence
- a punishing attitude toward self or others
- nightmares and sleep disturbances
- psychic numbing
- flatness of affect
- emotional constriction or blunting
- numbed and repressed feelings
- feelings of shame

- protecting others while ignoring yourself
- loyalty that is not deserved
- meaningless self-sacrifice
- the inability to protect yourself
- chronic anxiety
- numerous somatic complaints

Clues as to when abuse might have taken place may be found by looking at pictures in family albums. Prior to the abuse, you probably have pictures of yourself with lively sparkling eyes and a vibrant smile. After the abuse has taken place, eyes lose their sparkle, and a sad numbness often shows on the face.

If you were abused as a child, you may be someone whose developmental processes have been arrested, whose brainwaves are irregular, who scans the environment for any sign of danger (to fight or flee, escape or avoid), who feels powerless, helpless, emotionally crippled, totally vulnerable and dependent; who cannot feel safe alone, who is probably afraid of the dark, who feels a constant need for protection from someone else and whose only surviving memories may be of a self who was once intact.

You may remember once feeling safe and alive and normally functioning. For this lost part of your soul you enter the worst depression and nightmare of your life, for you may grieve forever the loss of your normally functioning self. Some authorities call this "soul murder." I do not believe the soul can be murdered—it can be lost, or hidden, and it can be rediscovered to bring you a new life.

Childhood abuse can splinter the personality into fragments, like a hammer smashing glass. Such a wounding renders the adult personality very vulnerable to external happenings. You can't concentrate or stay focused, because the various fragments are always pushing for attention. There is no inner peace.

A person with Dissociative Identity Disorder never knows who she's going to be or how she's going to feel. There is simply no continuity to life. Experiences don't carry over from one personality fragment to the next. If you suffer Dissociative Identity Disorder, you may treat people you have known for years as if you are meeting them for the first time. You may greet them warmly one time, coolly the next.

You automatically scan the environment to determine how to survive in it. "What do other people want from me?" You get so good at scanning, you can give other people what they want before they even know they want it. People pleasing and mind reading behavior becomes a coping device. You may think, "If I please you, then you will protect me." Outward display of anger and confrontation are avoided at all costs, so as not to trigger other's anger, and your own internal rage.

These behaviors are not choices. Once abuse becomes imprinted in the brain and on the cellular level, you're on "automatic pilot." I have known people who tried for years to change these behaviors and could not—until they learned the healing techniques which I will discuss later in the book.

Abuse victims form identity by attachments to others, especially those who are seen as protectors. You *are* someone's wife or husband, son or daughter, significant other, or a job title, (I'm an accountant), community (I'm a New Yorker), nation (I'm American), or cultural (I'm Indian), or political (I'm Republican), or even body weight (I'm fat).

People who wear designer shirts and jeans are searching for an identity. When they think they look *just right*, they relax and say, "I fit, I belong, I'm someone, I can be loved, I've found the American Dream, because *I look right*."

Inwardly, other feelings persist. They buy another outfit. They look in the mirror and think, *"this* is the right look." A new identity is born—and sometimes a compulsive spender. False identities become cemented and rigid, keeping the personality from growing and expanding. There is no access to the inner self, hidden behind walls.

Many people cannot remember what happened in their childhoods, particularly if it is painful or frightening. Without painstaking therapy to help recover the lost memories and feelings, much of the past may remain locked into closets of repression.

Those memories and feelings continue to affect the personality, however, and may show up in other, perhaps surprising and unwanted, forms. (Refer to symptoms listed on pages 40 & 41). The pattern of victimization may remain until all the repressed memories are recovered and understood.

Victimization can occur at any level. Doctors may even victimize their patients by prescribing drugs to "ease the pain," which addict the patients so they now have two problems instead of one. They are then told to go to twelve step meetings and admit they're addicts and they'll be OK. Another victimization.

I once worked in a chemical dependency unit at one of the most beautiful psychiatric hospitals in the country. When I allowed women to talk about their sexual abuse issues, I was ordered by the management to stop. "They are here to learn to cope with their addiction. That's all they can handle," I was told.

That hospital advertised its services as a dual diagnosis chemical dependency facility where patients could "work on their issues." Staff members, many of whom were terrified by their own untreated childhood abuse, refused to allow the treatment they professed to administer.

If you are taking drugs to suppress fear from abuse, facing the fear and dissolving it will help you not to succumb to the addiction. One of the main attractions to the addiction will be gone. In order to stop being a "victim," you must remember and confront your personal history. This usually takes the help of a therapist or treatment center. However, many therapists and treatment centers, even though they claim to offer assistance, cannot do so. Too many therapists are suffering from their own past abuse and are afraid of triggering their own deep fears from their past abuse.

In addition, there are other, even more malevolent reasons people are deceived and victimized by the institutions they turn to for help: Managed Care contracts. Hospitals and other treatment care centers advertise services in order to obtain insurance Managed Care contracts.

In order to secure the contract and the funding it provides, treatment facilities claim they are providing services that they actually are not. They do this by giving the insurance company a dual diagnosis for the patient. A dual diagnosis is given, but not the treatment for it. The insurance companies pay off and the patient doesn't get the service.

Patients may not know they're denied full services, because they don't read their insurance bill. Shop around for the services you need. When you find a therapist or treatment center to help you, make sure you get the services you pay for.

Insurance claims are made using the diagnoses listed in the American Psychiatric Association: *Diagnostic and Statistical Manual of Mental Disorders*, Fourth Edition (DSM IV). The DSM IV definition of Posttraumatic Stress Disorder indicates that the "stressor must occur outside the limits of ordinary human events." Who are they kidding?

One in three women are sexually abused in childhood. One in four women are raped. Four million women are beaten each year. Domestic violence, rape and sexual abuse are common occurrences in the lives of women.

Because childhood abuse leaves women with limited coping

defenses and compensated ego functions, many go on to be victims of rape, domestic violence, and misogynistic relationships.

Psychic trauma is hardly "outside the limits of human experience." But the American Psychiatric Association is still in denial about just how widespread and devastating childhood abuse actually is, and how continuously it impacts the lives of the victims.

Patients who pay good money for health insurance may be denied effective treatment because they cannot be properly diagnosed as having a Posttraumatic Stress Disorder or "childhood sexual abuse trauma" even though they have all the symptoms. One female patient was told by her doctor she couldn't possibly have a Posttraumatic Stress Disorder because she didn't serve in Viet-Nam!

Insurance companies also have their heads stuck in the sand. With the treatment limitations of managed care providers, only a person's surface issues can be addressed. Most managed care contracts require the therapist to make a report of the patient's progress every five to ten sessions. An insurance person who has never seen the patient determines when the patient has had enough therapy. The therapist is usually only given permission to treat the patient with medication and "brief therapy."

Brief therapy is ineffective for treatment of childhood abuse. It is tantamount to putting a bandage over a gaping wound. In fact, many managed care therapists refer to this type of treatment as "slap a bandage on it and send the patient out until the next crisis occurs."

If a patient can afford the cost of treatment, without resorting to insurance, it increases the chances of effective treatment. However, it takes a great deal of money to afford therapy when you pay out of your own pocket. Even if you can pay, there are numerous pitfalls to avoid, including inappropriate treatment, and revictimization.

SARAH

When Sarah was a small child, friends and neighbors whispered that someday, something terrible would happen to the Benjamin children. Speculation was made as to which of the children would end up dead from suicide, perhaps a car wreck or drug overdose. The Benjamins had divorced when Sarah was six, and they had agreed on joint custody of Sarah and her two brothers, Kevin and Scott. Mondays, Tuesdays and Thursdays, and part of Friday the children lived with their mother, Candice; Wednesdays, Friday evenings, Saturdays and Sundays were spent with their father, Bob.

It was apparent to everyone except the parents that the children were confused by the arrangement. The children called their father, "Mother," and their mother, "Father" when they arrived at the other's house. By the time the children figured out with which parent they were residing, it was time to switch again. The constant adjusting to new environments left them insecure.

You could say the children were victims from the start. Their parents misused them to get back at one another for their hurts from the marriage—and to meet their own needs instead of deciding what was best for the children. Candice assigned Sarah the task of being her best friend. She confided everything to Sarah, making Sarah feel responsible for her. Sarah tried to protect her mother; to take care of her and live up to her mother's expectations. Sarah quickly learned to feel like a failure and became hesitant to even try to ride her bicycle.

When Candice showed up drunk to car pool to school, other parents refused to allow their children to ride with her. Stories abound of Sarah and her brothers watching their mother engaging in sex with numerous men. Soon the neighborhood children were forbidden to play at or go into the large, palatial Benjamin home.

The father, Bob, knew what was going on. He thought about trying for custody and hired a detective. He also hired a nanny to live in Candice's home and care for the children. The nanny and detective supplied him with written documents of neglect and abuse by Candice. Later, Bob hid the letters after his mother told him the children needed a "good image" for a mother. Grandmother reasoned, "They're so young they won't ever remember this. They should think well of their mother."

Bob said the word *mother* with all the conviction of a man who decreed his own mother a saint. To him, *Motherhood* was a sacred institution full of images of apple pie and nurturing and all bountiful love.

During his own childhood, his mother had caught him peering through the key hole at his sister, Terri. Instead of scolding him or telling him to respect his sister's privacy, his mother took him to her room and proceeded to undress. She held his hands to her breasts and told him he never needed to look at another woman because she would give him everything he could ever want from a woman. All he needed to do was come to her.

Bob's father had become financially successful when oil was discovered on his thousand acre wheat and cattle ranch. He rewarded himself with extramarital affairs and flaunted them to the community. Bob's mother consoled herself by telling herself she was the wife of a wealthy man. She bought expensive jewelry and joined the country club.

For affection she turned to her son, Bob. She protected her bond to Bob by saying, "No woman is ever good enough for you." Bob, by the cross-generational bonding with his mother, became a victim of emotional and physical incest. In his later life he could not bond with any woman. His love remained loyal to his mother. If he ever wanted to become intimate with a woman, guilt feelings of disloyalty to his mother emerged. He quickly interrupted the intimacy to distance himself from the relationship. He did this by becoming abusive verbally, having an extramarital affair, or going on a drunken tirade. Then he could relax.

Bob married and divorced two women; but he never "divorced" the right woman, his mother. He used women as his mother had used him. He vented his rage at not receiving the love he needed from his mother by raging at other women. He verbally, physically, and sexually abused them. Bob was the typical man who hated women. He raped a deaf girl in his youth (she couldn't tell on him), had numerous affairs during his two marriages, and frequented whore houses (he even stole the money he had paid the prostitutes for their services). In his mind, he divided women into sexual objects (whores) and his sacred mother.

He wanted his little girl, Sarah, to fit his image of a daughter: sweet, helpless, and needing him. Sarah was smart, and quickly learned, using her assigned role, to manipulate her father. It was inconceivable for Bob to accept his daughter, or any other woman, as adequate, competent, and capable, with needs of her own, even though verbally that's what he said he wanted. The nonverbal communication and mixed messages he gave Sarah confused her.

When Sarah and her brothers had visitation with their father, he often played *Born Free*, and had them all sing the song together. He told them they were free to do anything they wanted to do. That translated into no discipline or proper guidance at his home. He taught them how to tend bar and mix his drinks and wait on him. Sarah was the designated "bar maid." Bob usually proceeded to get drunk in order to tolerate the noise of his children screaming and fighting each other. When he became irritated, he took off his belt and gave them a licking.

Bob thought his second wife, Beverly, would be a good mother figure and help him take care of his children. As Sarah approached young adulthood and began to mature and develop breasts, her father would stare at them. He also made inappropriate sexual gestures to his second wife, in his daughter's presence, such as putting his hands in her pants or in her bra. Beverly was concerned about Bob's sexual behavior in front of Sarah. She confronted Bob about it and also asked him to stop staring at Sarah's breasts.

When he didn't, Beverly went to Candice's psychiatrist and told him she was afraid that Bob would sexually molest Sarah. She intended for this information to be passed back to Candice, to be used for Sarah's protection. Years later, after Bob's second divorce, Sarah accused her father of raping her. He, of course, denied this, and everyone quickly rallied around him, saying Sarah must be crazy. That was only the beginning of Sarah's continued victimization.

Several months after Sarah went off to college in her shiny, new, red, sports car, she was forced off the road and raped. In her struggle to get free from her attacker, she was hit on the head by his gun, requiring seven stitches in her head. Two weeks prior, she had experimented with LSD, where she had experienced many frightening realizations about her family.

With few resources of her own to deal with her drug reactions, the rape threw her "over the edge." Sarah was admitted to a prestigious psychiatric hospital. Bob took her brothers to see her at her worst, to teach them a lesson not to take drugs.

For four, long years, Sarah was medicated. No improvement was made. She was transferred to another hospital with an even more prestigious reputation. There she was medicated for another four years with no improvement. She intermittently suffered bouts of depression, suicidal ideation, and paranoid delusions. Bob paid the $15,000 monthly expenses out of his own pocket, or Sarah would have been discharged. Because Sarah entered the hospital at nineteen years of age, the time when most young people are establishing an identity, Sarah formed an identity of a mental patient instead of a young woman taking and making her place in and with the world.

Bob and his second wife, Beverly, divorced, but Beverly continued to urge Bob to get Sarah out of the hospital and give her outpatient treatment. Instead of relying on medication to calm her, Sarah needed coping skills.

Sarah was victimized by her parents at an early age. She was used as a narcissistic object in their tug of war, sexually abused and betrayed by her father. Her protests were drowned out by the rest of her family and friends. Her rape revictimized her and so did the hospitals. She was hospitalized too long, and controlled with medication instead of receiving counseling and coping skills.

Both hospitals refused to offer Sarah services such as biofeedback, Posttraumatic Stress Disorder therapy, or head injury trauma retraining, because of the political infighting among hospital staff. The medical doctors refused to teach Sarah biofeedback so she could learn how to relax and control her own anxiety. The doctors ordered her to take medication, thereby keeping Sarah and her family dependent upon them to control Sarah's moods. The hospitals were equipped with exceptional biofeedback departments but Sarah was never referred to them.

When Beverly called the biofeedback department of the second hospital to request treatment for Sarah, she was told, "The medical doctors won't acknowledge us. They think they can do everything with medications." That hospital used Sarah and her father for a $15,000 monthly pay check.

The expense to the hospital of keeping a person decreases dramatically the longer they are in the hospital. Most of the money it takes to operate a hospital occurs in the first week of hospitalization. Insurance companies won't allow payment to go on indefinitely. Most people have short stays.

Bob had been told over and over by friends and by Beverly what was happening to Sarah. Bob did not heed the advice and only replied, "the doctors know best."

Sarah had been an exceptionally beautiful girl in her teen years, with long, straight, raven hair and black penetrating eyes. After years of victimization and medication, her eyes looked blank and hollow; her smile was gone. Forgotten, betrayed, and overmedicated, Sarah had no identity or will of her own. Her life was a living hell. She had no one to turn to except her father, Bob. She pleaded with him to take her home, and asked why he allowed her to be abused and neglected by her mother. Bob lied, and denied that he ever knew anything about the abuse. He did, however, finally take Sarah out of the hospital, and brought her home to live with him.

When Sarah left, the hospital threatened, "she'll kill herself." Bob replied, "If she does, she'll be better off than spending her life in a mental institution." That was several years ago. Since then, Sarah has lived at home with her father. She is enrolled in college and has made no suicide attempts. Her father reports she does experience some paranoid feelings, but those are fewer and farther between times, as she learns to cope, and establish an identity in the world at large.

Sarah will never be completely well until she remembers and deals with what really happened in her childhood. And everyone in her family has an enormous stake in that not happening.

Chapter Four

Victims Beliefs

A buse is the most destructive thing that can happen to a child. Abusive adults commonly perpetrate these injustices and injuries onto a small helpless child by treating the child as a narcissistic object, as if the child had no human rights at all. The child then incorporates into her psyche the same belief system and contempt for herself as the perpetrator. In adulthood, the abused may not only repeat the cycle of abuse, but continue to depreciate herself through self-abuse.

Childhood victims believe that whatever happens to them is their fault; this is imprinted on the brain and continues to affect them throughout life. People who have untreated childhood abuse issues may suffer a lifetime of guilt, low self-esteem, and depression. They truly believe they are worthless and have no rights.

From this core belief stems many branches of self-doubt about their ability to care and protect themselves. They believe they are guilty and responsible for the crimes perpetrated upon them. When they are treated as a worthless object, to be used and manipulated, they believe that's what they deserve. Because of the guilt they carry with them at all times, childhood victims are unable to feel differently about themselves, or learn from experience.

GUILT

Guilt is capable of arresting personality development. A child who is victimized and made to feel responsible and guilty cannot leave that psychological place until the conflict is resolved and integrated. Guilt stops emotional maturation.

If the personality is emotionally arrested at the age of four, then that person will be an emotional four year old for the rest of his or her life, or until the conflict is resolved. But other parts of the personality do go on and develop, such as the mental, spiritual and physical. You can be a successful attorney and run an entire corporation and still be an emotional four year old, constantly seeking reassurance and acceptance by having extra marital affairs.

The biggest mistake people make in trying to overcome emotional conflicts is to reason their way out. This doesn't work. Logic and reason are intellectual processes.

Emotional problems need to be felt and worked through emotionally to be resolved. An old saying many therapists quote is, "You can't heal it if you can't feel it." These beliefs, and the emotional conflicts and issues that arise from them, can be overcome by doing inner child work, positive visualizations, and affirmations with the help of a skilled therapist. Many therapists are skilled in assisting abused people find their center of wellness and wholeness.

Victimization begins much earlier than the actual abuse. All family members participate in the abuse cycle that is handed down generation after generation due to the attitudes and beliefs generated in the family.

In a family, behavior is patterned—the behavior of one family member influences and is influenced by other family members. Your beliefs are shaped by the family you grew up in.

Family beliefs that make the ground fertile for abuse include:
- women and children are second class citizens
- children should be seen but not heard
- children have no choice but to mind adults
- living for others is the way to be
- you can't make it on your own
- loyalty to the family means survival
- men are superior, women are inferior (male privilege)
- belief in patriarchal ideology
- rigid adherence to the traditional roles of men and women
- rigid specifications for "how families should be"
- a belief they are happy and superior to others (myth of the happy family)
- your self-worth is based on self-denial
- expect to take care of others but do not expect to take care of yourself or to be nurtured by others

Such beliefs are very powerful and help determine attitudes, judgments, and perceptions. They play a big role in determining how you react to situations.

When you have been abused in childhood you have no idea how to protect yourself from being used or victimized by others. Being used feels normal. It leaves you prey for further revictimization. Victim beliefs add up to insurmountable feelings of hopelessness, guilt, low self-esteem, despair, powerlessness, helplessness and depression.

In abusive families, the group is maintained at the expense of the individual. Differences of opinion are discouraged. Children have few friends outside the family. They grow up isolated from the outside world. Because most of their time is spent at home, they develop poor social skills. This increases the isolation. These beliefs are the underpinning of a "victim life-style" characterized by feelings of powerlessness and passive behavior.

Vicious cycles of behavior can be perpetuated from these beliefs. For example, parents who have been sexually abused in their own childhoods look to their children for the love and affection they didn't get. They use their children to meet their needs for love and acceptance instead of meeting those needs of the children.

Small children are completely dependent on their parents, and since their parent's caring is essential for existence, children do all they can to avoid losing their parent's love and protection. From the very first day onward, he will muster all his resources to this end, like a small plant that turns toward the sun in order to survive (Miller, 1979, 1994).

Some emotionally insecure mothers condition their children in a particular way. They are able to hide their insecurity from their children and everyone else behind a hard, authoritarian, domineering facade. But their children have an amazing ability to intuitively perceive and take on the role subconsciously assigned to them. This role secures "love" for the children—that is, his parents' exploitation (Miller, 1979, 1994). The children are conditioned to need to be needed.

These children later function as "mothers" to their mothers as confidantes, comforters, advisers, and supporters. They may take on some of the responsibility for their siblings and eventually develop a special sensitivity to the needs of others. It is no wonder, in their adult life so many of these individuals become social workers, nurses, psychologists and other allied helping professionals.

This type of upbringing can lead to the *as if* personality. The *as if* person develops in such a way that she does only what is expected of her and remains unaware of how much more there is to her.

She cannot find her true self because she cannot live it. She complains of emptiness, futility, and feels partly dead inside. She becomes extremely vulnerable to sexual abuse because she is geared to give whatever others want from her. When her perpetrator turns to her for power and control, and for the unconditional, nonthreatening love that only a child can provide, she is an easy victim.

Abusive parents are self-centered and self-serving toward their children. They unconsciously deny their children individuation and maturation. Their children are never to succeed in life more than they, or to become adequate and able to function without them. Their children are to stay immature adults, so the parents can continue to be needed and run their children's lives.

Abused children bond to their parents in an extremely traumatic, unhealthy way. They usually continue to be dependent upon their parents long after they are grown, still seeking the love and approval that is never forthcoming.

In a patriarchal family, where the man is the head of the house and his power extends over everyone in it, he believes he has the right to have *all* his needs met, regardless. If his wife is unavailable for sex or nurturing, he turns to his female daughters and presses them into service. "It's my way or the highway."

RIGID RULES

Feelings are spawned from the thoughts that come from beliefs. Rigid rules are then put into place in the family setting to enforce the family beliefs. These rigid rules are easily identified by the words *should, ought, must, always* encoded in the family commandments. Blind obedience to these rules leads to destructive, self-defeating, behavior. Some family rules are spoken. Others are implied, but never stated out loud. They exist below the level of awareness.

Some common unspoken rules include: "don't lead your own life," "always ask me for approval for everything you do," "protect your parents' feelings or image," "don't talk back to your parents," "always look good," "you *should* make us proud," or "act normal no matter how mixed up or crazy you feel!"

Children in abusive homes are not allowed to develop separate identities and individuation. The rigid rules are reinforced by the children being assigned labels. Children may be assigned a label of the good child, or the bad child, or hero, scapegoat, quiet child, or the funny one.

These labels serve several purposes. On the surface, they create an illusion of security and belonging in the family. Covertly, they insure that the children will remain immature and dependent upon their parents. The labels protect the parents roles as needed and all powerful because they deny their children the emotional growth to surpass them. They child with a label will always wear that label, never outgrow it or be allowed to change it. The true person within the child will be denied. The power of the loyalty to the family system may be so strong that to break a family rule is to evoke tremendous guilt.

The distortion in your belief system is furthered when you think, *it never happened; I made it all up. That could never happen in my family.* You start doubting your ability to perceive reality correctly. You depend upon someone else to do your thinking for you because you can't trust your own thought processes. Because your thoughts and feelings are so painful, they are usually repressed, along with memories of childhood abuse.

· · ·

Many of your feelings, such as anger, may have been unacceptable while you were growing up. So you learned to repress them. Repressed anger and rage hurt you. Just because the feelings are not felt does not mean they go away. They manifest in painful, sometimes life threatening and devastating symptoms. Symptoms then replace the painful repressed feelings, trying to tell the story of what actually happened.

When victimized, men and women react differently. Most often, men externalize and women internalize, what happens to them. For this reason, women develop symptoms of depression, or headaches, and go to doctors. Men act out, commit violent crimes, get drunk, and end up in jail.

Your outlook on life is forever changed by childhood abuse. Sexual childhood abuse destroys the normally functioning capacity to enjoy life. Because you develop a rigid set of attitudes and rules in order to cope, a great deal of mental flexibility is lost. You may fail to grow as a person. You may identify with the aggressor thinking and viewing life in terms of *power over*, rather than possessing the *power to be*.

Most sexual childhood abuse is a result of the hostile attempts of men to establish their sense of power, domination and subjugation over females. Female children are victimized ten times more than male children. A female child who has been victimized is likely to quickly accept her position of inferiority, and learns to be submissive and acquiesce to the wishes of men. She even looks to a man to protect her because she thinks women cannot protect themselves.

But a female child will not accept that anything is wrong with her unless she has been brainwashed and damaged in this way. Men who want to establish their dominance and superiority initiate women into inferiority when they are young, weak, and vulnerable.

Abusers usually pick on the weakest family member they can find. The more vulnerable the child, the less chance there is that the abuser will be caught. The injured young child is duped by the perpetrator into thinking it was all her fault that she was hurt, scared, humiliated and defiled. The perpetrator may accuse a three year old of coming on to him and blame her for the sexual abuse.

Threats from the abuser reinforce the secret. The child accepts the responsibility, guilt for the victimization, and for keeping her injury a secret. The emotional scars can last a lifetime. In my private practice, and also at psychiatric hospitals where I worked, approximately eighty percent of all people I saw had been sexually victimized in childhood.

Because victims have numbed and repressed feelings, and don't trust what feelings they do have, they are unable—even as adults—to sense when danger is present. They remain incredibly naive. Being used and abused may feel normal.

The self-destructive belief system, which originated with the victimization, further weakens them and leaves sexually abused children prey for later revictimization.

Attitudes stemming from sexual childhood abuse
- I need a man to protect me
- I need a man to take care of me
- I need a man to save me
- I need a man to make me respectable
- I am nothing without a man
- I am helpless, powerless, hopeless, guilty, dirty
- I am worthless, bad, tainted, flawed, a mistake, unlovable
- I have no choices
- No one would want me if they knew
- I am a failure, a whore, bitch, prostitute
- I am shamed, weak, never good enough
- I have to be perfect at all costs
- I must always be pleasant
- I protect men's feelings, and never say no
- I sacrifice myself at all costs for love and approval
- If I do everything just right, I'll be loved
- If I don't get angry, I'll be loved
- I minimize any cruelties or slights
- I must always smile and be congenial
- Others will take care of me if I'm nice
- I must always say and do the right things
- If I give him (sex) anything he wants, he'll stay around
- I am either passive or aggressive, but not assertive
- I fail to set boundaries and protect myself
- I fail to be assertive and take up for myself
- I use avoidance as a coping skill
- I think others know what's best for me

- I want others to take care of me, emotionally and financially
- I intellectualize anything that happens
- I put walls up around myself so no one will know
- If someone doesn't punish me, I'll punish myself
- I'll exercise myself to death to have the perfect body to gain approval from others
- I deny or minimize unpleasant things

Ironically, even though you may have panic attacks, flashbacks, and nightmares or constantly scan the environment to flee from danger, you think, *it never happened; I made it all up. That couldn't happen in my family. I came from a good family.* Self-protective behaviors and limit setting were extinguished while abuse was taking place.

Instead, you act as if these behaviors are foreign to you. They don't exist as an option. In abusive households, self-protection and limit setting are not role modeled. As one patient put it, "I learned from my mother that females devalued themselves and gave away all their self-respect in order to have a relationship with a man."

The lack of perceived choices traps you by circumstances in abusive relationships. Because you see no way out, it is easy to spiral into long term depressions and feelings of helplessness and worthlessness. You may even attempt suicide. You have learned to offer yourself as a sacrifice because that's the way you survived. When that no longer works, suicide seems like the only alternative.

It is easy to ignore the one person who can really help you. You can protect yourself by the choices you make and what you allow to influence you. Coping skills such as assertiveness and choosing a conscious awareness are available through relearning.

Conscious choice, assertiveness and self-protectiveness can be learned as an adult. Even though the nurturing protectiveness of mother or father was not there for you as a powerless child, you can learn to cope as an adult. The first step is to stop believing you are helpless and accept your power.

VICTIM NO MORE

Chapter Five

Myth
Of The
Happy Family

Parents have the "power of God" over their helpless and dependent children. And to most young children, God looks a lot like mom or dad. Many parents think they own their children, and treat them accordingly, like any other possession. Society supports the belief that children belong to their parents and that the parent is always right.

Any society that treats any class of its citizens as property, whether they are black, poor, disabled, women, or children, creates a social framework that is geared to perpetuating patterns of violence and sexual abuse (Lew,1988).

Of those who abuse their children, this belief of *children as property* is most strongly found in fundamentally religious, traditional, and paternalistic families. It is this attitude of possession that sets the stage for abuse.

A patriarchal society fosters the idea—sometimes reinforced by law—that a husband has a "right" to receive sex. Many male perpetrators have attempted to use their wife's unavailability to rationalize and justify abusive behavior.

For centuries the family has been enshrined as the bulwark of society. The family has had the sanction of Christianity since early times, and has developed enormous legal standing. English law, for many years, applied the *Rule of Thumb* for men disciplining their wives and children. The Rule stated that men were to use a rod no bigger around than their thumb, to beat their wives and children.

Society has always done its best to create the image of the perfect family. Many people, due to cultural and societal expectations of a happy childhood, idealize their family and deny the reality of what actually happened while they were growing up.

It is a sacred societal belief (sacred cow) that fathers and mothers love their children and know what's best for them. In turn, children are supposed to love and obey their parents. Television shows, magazines, and movies, create images of caring and nurturing parents meeting their children's needs for guidance, love and affection.

With all the societal expectations of a "golden childhood," you may be tempted to rewrite history and create a fantasy life of your childhood, and then believe it. "Of course, I had a happy childhood. It was just like *Leave it to Beaver*."

When family and parents are idealized, what happens to the negatives? The weakest, most vulnerable child, the one most unable to rebel, is scapegoated and ascribed the task of incorporating the negative values of the family. That child is sacrificed to preserve the image of the "good family" by becoming the "bad" child. That child then becomes the "sewer" for the rest of the family, the dump for the family's unacceptable attributes. The parent or family continues to appear "perfect," and the child is "always wrong, bad, dumb, selfish, or mean." The child takes on this negative image to protect the parent's "good" image and preserve the "basic goodness" of the family.

BEVERLY

Remember Bob Benjamin from Chapter Three? Bob's second wife, Beverly, came for counseling during their stormy seven year marriage. Beverly was obviously intelligent and highly attractive but suffered from extreme insecurity and couldn't trust her own perceptions. She thought she was ugly and stupid. In talking about her childhood, she mentioned that her mother had repeatedly told her she was mean, so mean that she had horns growing out of her head. After years of being told she was mean enough for horns, Beverly parted her hair looking for them.

During her adolescence, her mother often told Beverly that she would give her $100 to leave home. She also threatened to turn her over to the authorities to be put in a state home for out-of-control children. Beverly usually replied to her mother, "You're my parent. You have to rear me until I'm eighteen," but inwardly she constantly feared being put out on the street. Beverly couldn't see where she was mean and out of control, and it bothered her.

At school, she made the honor roll, was popular and held class offices. She worked hard to be a good person and a dutiful daughter. One might say she was an ideal child. Like Snow White, Beverly couldn't understand that her real offense was being more intelligent and attractive than her mother. Beverly couldn't see her mother's jealousy because she believed she was mean and bad. When Beverly entered therapy, she was still working hard to gain her mother's approval. She believed her mother really loved her. After all, she reasoned, "mothers love their children, don't they?"

Bob repeated this double-bind pattern with Beverly. She thought he loved her, when he was really rejecting her. As a child, Beverly had been given the unspoken message from her mother, "Your feelings are not important. I'm the only one who counts." Deprived of adequate time, attention, and care as a child, when Beverly came for counseling, she felt invisible. She had learned to deny her own existence.

DENIAL

Denial is one of the most primitive and powerful of the psychological defenses in its struggle to normalize craziness in a dysfunctional family. The myth of the happy family uses denial when it tells us what is considered normal and acceptable. It fosters an ideal of unconditional parental love. On the other hand, fairy tales such as Rose Red, Snow White, and Hansel and Grethel tell us about the shadow side, where wicked step mothers attempt to kill the children and where fathers abandon them.

One of the hardest tasks to face in therapy is uncovering what early family life was really like. You know what childhood is supposed to be like; you may use denial when you imagine happy scenes of carefree play and unconditional love.

The ugly scenes are repressed. They may be difficult and painful to recall. Recollection is a vital step in therapy. In fact, finding your own truth is one of the most important things you can do for yourself on your road to recovery.

POWER AND CONTROL

In families where children are victimized, parents frequently act *as if* they are perfect and the children are second class citizens. These families are further distinguished by one parent playing a dominant role, while the other parent is submissive, as if in a master - slave coupling.

The dominance - submission pattern is replayed in different verses throughout the family. Someone is in power and controls the other. The head of the house, in an attempt to control others, may become a petty tyrant or demigod. In paternalistic families, usually the father is in power and controls the mother, who is submissive.

She, in turn, has power over, and controls, the children. Within the power group of the children, the stronger may control and abuse the weaker. The weakest one kicks the dog. Power is seen as *power over*, not the *power to be* (empowerment).

In the abusive family environment, the exercise of parental power is arbitrary, capricious, and absolute. Rules are erratic, inconsistent, or patently unfair (Herman 1992).

Control may be established and maintained through physical abuse by whippings or slaps, or by constant criticism, belittling, or humiliation. The parent who uses criticism as a means of control, will find something to criticize, no matter what the child does. The child could be punished for smirking or simply the look on her face. Dancing at the end of the parents' emotional string becomes a way of life, not a choice.

ISOLATION

Families where abuse occurs tend to isolate themselves from other relationships. Parents may be critical of their children's friends or not allow the children to associate with others outside the family. The flow of information coming into the family unit is restricted. Outside sources of protection are cut off.

With only limited knowledge available to them, children are conditioned to think what is happening at home is normal. You may be told, "your family members are the only people who will ever care about you." A parent may be intrusive, invade your privacy, and routinely go through your drawers.

Family members may be so thoroughly intimidated by the controlling parent that they are unable to support one another. All information must pass through the controller. Direct communication between other family members is stopped by means of coercion, disapproval, threats, or pacts of secrecy. The secrecy further isolates you.

You may know something is wrong, but can't tell what it is. There is no one to turn to for help, understanding, and comfort. The very people who are supposed to protect you are the ones causing you pain.

With no way to dispel your painful feelings, and no one to validate them, you feel different from others, which furthers the isolation. Faced with chronic psychic pain, you numb your fearful feelings through repression, addiction, or some type of compulsive behavior. This creates an inner emptiness upon which you build a facade and pretend everything is "just fine."

Everyone else in the family is manipulated by the controller(s) through humiliation, belittling or brute force, to think and feel the same way. Differences are strongly discouraged.

Even though abused children grow up and leave home, they

are likely to remain emotionally immature and repeat the cycle for the next generation. All this is accomplished by mixed messages, manipulation and guilt. "We want you to be happy." "We want you to succeed." You hear the words burdened by a martyred tone of voice and body language that says, "you better not do better than I."

The reality is, parents do not love you if they cannot accept you for yourself, but instead try and make you into what they want you to be. This alienates you from your real self. You are used in selfish ways, tormented, demeaned, humiliated, and told, "this is for your own good." People who truly love you want the best for you. They want you to mature and become independent.

When you are forced to be something other than what you are, enormous compensations in the way of mental perceptions and feelings occur. You learn to distort reality, numb your feelings or simulate the acceptable feelings in order to "fit in."

Members of an abusive family are connected to each other through a fantasy that they trust, love and care about each other. The caring is not reality based and the actual emotional climate is cold. Children become emotionally deprived. They starve for affection, while frozen smiles and forced laughter give the pretense that they are loved.

Abandonment is a constant threat to your security, because if you see through the illusions, you will be "cast out." This cannot be stated strongly enough. It takes on the aspect of a life and death situation. If you dare see through the facade and charade of your family, you must face your own feelings of not being loved and accepted as the unique individual you are. You suffer pain from the realization that your life is a lie.

Growing up in this kind of environment is difficult and requires many ego compensations. Judith Herman, in *Trauma and Recovery*, tells about the child's dilemma, "Double Think."

The child must find a way to form primary attachments to caretakers who are either dangerous or, from her perspective, negligent. She must find a way to develop a sense of basic trust and safety with parents who are untrustworthy and unsafe. She must develop a sense of self in relation to others who are helpless, uncaring or cruel. She must develop a capacity for bodily self-regulation in an environment in which her body is at the disposal of others' needs, as well as a capacity for self-soothing in an environment without solace. She must develop the capacity for initiative in an environment which demands that she bring her will into complete conformity with that of her abuser. Ultimately, she must develop a capacity for intimacy out of an environment where all intimate relationships are corrupt, and an identity out of an environment which defines her as a whore and a slave.

When you deny your feelings and perceptions of reality in order to belong, you play "the charade of the normal family." It is almost impossible to develop a strong sense of self-confidence if you must constantly lie about what you are thinking and feeling. There might as well be an elephant in the living room that everyone pretends is not there. All the while, you are getting molested, used as mother's best friend, and denying that your needs aren't getting met.

You probably feel guilty that you have needs at all. You are afraid to ask for affection, warmth, and understanding. To maintain the illusion of parental love, you may avoid seeing how your parents really feel about you. You may decide to maintain the illusion rather than accept a reality filled with rejection and pain. As Alice Miller says in her book *Banished Knowledge*, "My hope was that if I needed nothing and sacrificed my life for others, surely I would eventually be given that love. But love cannot be earned, whether by self-denial or by altruistic service. It is either given at birth, or it isn't."

When parents use their children to meet their own desires instead of meeting their children's needs, they view the children's needs as tiresome and irrelevant. The children are placed in the role of giving, but they don't receive. The imbalance of power is tremendous.

Emotionally deprived children cannot see their parents' faults; instead, they blame themselves and think they are bad. The illusion of their mothers as being good and loving is preserved at the expense of their own feelings of worth. When parents are idealized in an effort to protect the ideal of family goodness, strength and protection, the child must assume all the faults. To abusive parents, children are expendable.

Abused children often grow into adulthood without emotionally having been children, or ever knowing their own feelings as separate from their parent's needs. This leaves them devoid of a sense of self or the ability to protect themselves. In fact, some children are taught they have *no right* to protect themselves, so self-protective behavior is completely foreign. They grow up vulnerable to abuse and exploitation from not just family members, but all others as well. Abused children alter their reality testing to adjust to a world where "abusive behavior is acceptable but telling the truth about it is sinful."

JANA

Jana's short, black hair fell over her downcast face as she told me what had happened in her life. Her arms hung lifeless from her shoulders. She looked like a Raggedy Ann doll you could bend in any position. She seemed unaware of her body or her sexuality. Her body language spelled, *learned helplessness*.

Jana's parents divorced when she was two years old. From that time on, she lived with her mother and her mother's numerous boyfriends. She was moved in and out of the boyfriend's homes; from state to state, and from continent to continent. Jana felt she was in the way and shoved aside. She was. Her mother told her to act happy and be nice to the boyfriends. She did.

Jana tried very hard to be good so her mother would notice her. But her mother was too caught up in her own life to relate to Jana. Instead, they discussed what her mother would wear on her dates and how she would fix her hair. Jana said with great pride, "Mother dates rich men. They take her on expensive trips."

When Jana was sixteen, she became involved with a twenty-two year old man. Her mother told her to go and live with him because she didn't have room for her anymore. She did. The relationship lasted a month. Jana was out on the street, became promiscuous, and addicted to drugs. She felt suicidal and crazy. In an effort to save herself, she called her father, who sent her money to come and live at his house. She got off drugs and entered therapy.

She idealized her mother whom she described as her "best friend" because they talked about all her mother's problems. It was very difficult for Jana to understand that her mother had not taken adequate care of her, and had not even met her most basic needs. Jana felt guilty for even having needs and felt she had been a great burden to her mother. She realized through therapy that it was her legal *right* to be cared for and nurtured.

When she gave up emotionally on her mother, she entered a profound depression and grieved for the loss of her mother's fantasy love. "I feel like I am some kind of horrible person," Jana wiped the tears from her eyes, "saying all these things about my mother. But, it's so weird that all of that could have been going on and I never realized it. What I was doing was dangerous. Mother didn't even care. I know that now. What's really weird though . . . I feel as if I've actually killed my mother." Jana stopped dissociating as she felt her pain. Soon after, she got a job and moved to her own apartment.

One night, quite startled, she sat up in bed, and a part of herself seemed to slip back into her body. She commented on how strange it felt, but for the first time, she felt whole. Jana was still emotionally very young, but now she was maturing and learning to love and protect herself. Best of all, Jana could now trust that her perceptions were true. She had succeeded in a parentectomy from her mother, and she had survived.

VICTIM NO MORE

Chapter Six

Violence Against Women

When Beverly met Bob Benjamin she thought she had found the most wonderful man in the world. He seemed perfect: handsome, charming, with black piercing eyes. His clean shaven face and curly black hair, his muscular, though small framed athletic body, entranced her.

Beverly was even more delighted by his three "darling" children who so desperately needed a responsible mother. She wanted to be the woman to take care and love them. She thought her son, Chris, from her former marriage and Bob's three children could all become one happy family. Beverly had heard the stories about Candice's drunken escapades. She felt sorry for Bob and his children.

Beverly thought all she had to do was love Bob to heal him from his scars. But some scars don't heal, they just make you tougher and harder—and meaner. That was for Beverly to find out during the next seven years as her knight in shining armor rusted into tin.

When Beverly married Bob, she was confident, full of life, with a twinkle in her brown eyes. When she left, her hair had turned a dull gray, eyes were hollowed by fear, and a psychotic depression stalked her soul. She had come to counseling to find out what she had done wrong in the marriage.

While she recounted what had taken place during the marriage, it was shocking that she could believe it was her fault. Bob was an old testament man who believed it was his right as a husband to make all the rules and all the decisions. His rules could change at a moment's notice. They were to suit his mood and his convenience only.

Bob moved into her house and sold his own. She watched in disbelief as Bob and his children dismantled her furniture, walls, and doors with axes, drills and hammers. He refused to allow her to discipline his children. Bob encouraged his children in antisocial behavior. He laughed when his youngest son chased Beverly with his penis in hand trying to piss on her. Disciplining his children consisted of occasional beatings when Bob was tired and had had enough.

One day Bob came in mad, kicked a door, walked down the

hall to the bedroom and kicked another hole in that door. His youngest son, followed the path of destruction kicking the same doors, trying the make as big a hole in them as his father had.

When Beverly complained and asked him to repair the damages, she was told "forget it and shut up." She thought she would teach Bob a lesson to respect property by having a lumber yard restore the doors with solid wood and send the bill to Bob. Bob was mad because of the bill, but didn't bother to read what the repairs were for. He went home and kicked the doors again, but this time he almost broke his foot and hand. That was the last of his damage to the property.

Bob drank more and more. Beverly pleaded with him to stop and join AA. Beverly thought the problems in the marriage were related to Bob's alcohol abuse. Beverly hoped she could have her charming, lovable, husband back if he would just stop drinking. She thought that would happen if she would just try harder. She invested time, energy, and money in this endeavor, but instead of Bob's changing, Beverly conditioned herself into *learned hopefulness*.

Inwardly, she felt all control over her life slipping away. She felt trapped. Bob had all the power. He put Beverly down and demeaned her constantly. He said, "You're getting old, your age is showing in your face. I'm rich and handsome. I deserve someone young and beautiful." Beverly was miserable, but she colored her hair and bought a new dress, nevertheless. By this time, she felt grateful Bob would stay with her at all.

The degradation eventually made Beverly feel like an untouchable with no rights who Bob would reward or punish according to his drunken moods. The times of peace, intermixed with the unpleasantness, addicted Beverly to Bob. Her preoccupation with Bob's behavior and what she could do to change it took all her time and energy. She lost her own existence.

The violence escalated. He began slapping and pushing Beverly around. He jerked the telephone out of her hand whenever she talked on it. He refused to allow her friends to visit in her home. He said he didn't like them. She became angry and told Bob to stop treating her with condescension.

In retaliation, he raped her. Her nine year old son heard her screaming. Chris walked into the bedroom with his twenty-two rifle. "Sgt. First Class reporting for duty," he saluted. "Do you want me to shoot him, Mother?" Beverly shuddered in horror as her son witnessed the violence. Bob quickly settled down and Beverly asked Chris to leave. Later that night, while she was sleeping, Bob brutally hit her. Beverly woke up in fright. Bob said he had been dreaming he was spanking one of his children. He denied any violence on his part.

Beverly couldn't understand why she couldn't get through to Bob. She thought it was her responsibility to hold the family together. She thought she must be communicating poorly and tried harder to communicate. She didn't want another divorce. She couldn't admit another mistake, especially where she felt she was being made a fool.

When they married, Bob had asked Beverly to stop working and stay home to take care of his children. She compromised and cut back her work to do so.

She had also made investments in other businesses. He told her the investments had to stop, because "no wife" of his would make him look less of a man among his business associates. After she grudgingly agreed to stop her investments to keep harmony in the marriage, Bob put her on a tight budget. Beverly was furious. "I'll make it up to you later," he said.

Beverly tried being assertive. She made "I" statements, such as, "I am very hurt by your physically pushing me around. I want you to stop and treat me with respect." His response was to deny she was ever hurt, then push her even harder, or shove her into a wall. Beverly was intimidated by his physical power and anger, and quickly learned the only thing Bob responded to favorably was to please him.

After years of brutal treatment and exhausting failures at communication with Bob, Beverly realized there was nothing she could do to improve things. She was sick from the stress. She was so run down she worried she might die of a disease like cancer. It was obvious Bob wanted her dependent upon him, and she begged him to meet even the simplest of her needs. He just laughed and refused. She couldn't understand why he didn't show any remorse for his actions or caring for her feelings. He confused her by always saying he loved her and then doing terrible and unloving things.

Beverly talked of divorce. Bob drew his gun on her and told her he would kill her if she got an attorney. She continued to try and "fix" the marriage. Bob now openly flaunted his affairs, and even brought one of his girlfriends into the house to meet Beverly. Bob also embarrassed Beverly in public by flirting with other women.

Bob drank too much when they went to restaurants, became unruly, pinched waitresses, and made caustic remarks to the service personnel. They were frequently asked to leave and soon were barred from almost every restaurant in the city, once at gun point. Then Bob would take Beverly home and leave again to spend the night somewhere else. Beverly would stay home and take care of his children.

One evening Bob came home and announced he was being sued by a business partner. He said he wanted Beverly to hear it first from him. In his own business, which was separate from his family ranching business, he had three partners. He had bought one partner out, but not before an investment was bought which made $3,000,000.00 the first year. Bob and his second partner had kept the investment a secret from the third, who lived out of state. They bought the third partner out without letting him know about it. The third partner suspected some such trick and sued. Bob laughed and said, "Good old Harry thinks he caught us, but he sued us on the wrong deal!"

Beverly knew she had to find a way out. She knew he could divorce her, but she was afraid to divorce him because of his threats to kill her. She did everything he wanted. She took all his humiliating abuse and asked him what she could do better to make him happy. She knew Bob had to think he had all the power and control, or he might eventually kill her. One night, Beverly stole Bob's keys to his office, slipped in, and took the information that proved the third partner's right to a share of the profits.

Bob asked for a divorce when it was no longer fun to abuse Beverly. Again, he threatened to kill her if she got an attorney. This time Beverly was ready, and told Bob, "I left the investment papers with an attorney. If anything happens to me, he has orders to send them, and my notarized testimony, to your ex-partner." Bob asked her what she wanted. She asked for a new house since his children had ruined hers. He agreed. She picked out a new, expensive home. Bob paid cash.

Bob said that even though they were going to be divorced, he still wanted to live with her when it was convenient for him. Beverly said she thought it was a good idea. The divorce papers were signed. Bob had decided on everything. Beverly didn't even have a divorce attorney. All she was concerned for was her life.

When Bob came over to her new house for his "privileges," Beverly told him he had treated her like a whore while they were married, so now she wanted to be paid for her services. She told him she wanted $100.00 an hour for every hour he was in the house. When Beverly convinced him she was serious, Bob left.

Beverly was relieved, but because of the years of abuse and fright, she remained emotionally unstable for some time. However, she understood that she had made a healthy choice. Every night as she slipped into bed, she said, "Thank you, God, for allowing me to live in peace."

The next four years, Beverly pieced her life back together. She was disheartened and depressed, as she had been taught that marriage is the most important thing in a woman's life. She missed "being married" and the status that marriage carried. But she welcomed her freedom and independence, with a new found respect for women and what abuse can do to anyone.

• • •

People once thought battered women were masochists (people who take pleasure in pain) and stayed in abusive relationships because they enjoyed the pain. That kind of thinking is out of touch with women's reality.

Battered women are prisoners of war in their own homes. Abusive men use violence in a deliberate and conscious way to gain power and control over women. The more intimidated, frightened and humiliated the woman becomes, the easier it is to control her. Physical, sexual, and psychological violence help him gain power over her.

One in three marriages has at least one violent act, from shoving to killing. Violence within marriages is increasing, but the cause for this remains complicated. No one single cause shows up as the reason for today's increased violence. It is a combination of causes; perhaps the violence we all see on TV and the changing roles of men and women in our society. At least fifty percent of batterers and their wives/partners have some history of child abuse in their backgrounds.

Battering behavior is about the abuse of power and control. As women make strides in gaining independence—working outside the home, learning to stand on their own and making their own decisions—the backlash has taken its toll. Abusive men use the patriarchal philosophy of male dominance and superiority to justify violence against women, i.e. keep them in line, subservient, under control, submissive, passive, and compliant.

Ironically, when a women asserts her independence, protects her children, and refuses to live as a prisoner under tyrannical conditions, she is most apt to be battered, maimed or killed. As women break the shackles of oppression, the violence against them is escalating into epidemic proportions. Domestic violence is the leading cause of injuries to women. Refer to the Appendix for statistics of injuries to women.

Several things make it possible for domestic violence to occur. No woman knowingly enters into a relationship where she will ultimately be ridiculed, controlled, humiliated, beaten, and possibly killed.

CONDITIONING

Some women gravitate toward violent relationships. Their abusive childhoods condition them to accept abuse as normal. The men they pick often resemble their abusive parent. The women already have low self-esteem, feel unworthy and guilty. They don't think they deserve better treatment.

The attraction toward an abuser is part of the pattern imprinted on the brain at an early age to repeat the trauma. Each time the abuse occurs, she hopes things will be different. She hopes the abuser will change. This hope overrides all her experiences, as she conditions herself into *learned hopefulness*.

Because of the conditioned *learned helplessness* and the

victim role she already plays, she feels ineffective in doing anything about the situation. Her responsibility of keeping the family together is one of her highest held values. She is an expert at selflessness and long suffering, traits she regards as admirable. Due to the constant eroding away of her confidence, she doesn't feel she can make it on her own.

WOMEN'S SOCIALIZATION

Women are historically socialized into self-sacrificing and passive, submissive behavior. Anger and assertiveness are discouraged, leaving women little option but to internalize their anger and pain. Many women are already conditioned into *learned helplessness* and *learned hopefulness* (hopefulness born of despair) from their past abuses, causing them depression and feelings of worthlessness. Feeling they have no active control over their lives, abused women can only hope it will get better, see psychics to predict the future, and hope it will be different.

A woman socialized into the "appropriate feminine behavior" is subservient to dominant men. As a child, she was probably also trained to accept violence and/or unhappiness as an unavoidable "given" in intimate relationships. She, therefore, lacks the coping skills necessary to make independent and self-protective judgements and decisions.

When women embody the "feminine principle," they are forced into a one sided oppressive development: they deny their masculine side and project it outward onto men. A woman only stands where a man's shadow falls. A "feminine" woman is truly half a person, and a masculine man is truly only half a man. He denies his feminine energies, and projects them outward onto women. So when these two stereotyped ideals find each other, they unite and desperately try to make a whole person. Being shackled together in this way, is like trying to run a three-legged race, where the partners each have a leg tied together. They run, stumble and fall, and sometimes crawl, to the finish line. Watching and participating in three-legged races is fun, but it's enough to convince even the most doubting person that indeed, one can make it better on her own than tied to an image partner.

Women are defined by the male oriented, patriarchal society, as daughters, virgins, mothers, and whores. They are denied power and receive power only secondarily from the benefits these roles provide. In these fragmented roles, women look for their identity through their relativeness to others—they don't even own their own existence.

This type of relatedness carries with it a nonassertive body posture that says, "You can take advantage of me." "You know more than I do." "Don't pay any attention to me." "Don't take me seriously." "I'm insufficient without a man." The body posture may be irregular, with the head tilted to one side. The head tilt, once thought attractive for women, is a historic sign of submission.

A woman is taught a man will protect and take care of her. Status and self-esteem are gained through an attachment to a powerful male. Her behavior becomes mindless "how to catch a husband" tactics. She focuses on building up a man's ego so he can live up to his image of manhood.

The image is impossible to live up to, causing him to feel inadequate. Reality is nevertheless denied, for the illusions of a patriarchal society. She takes care of his feelings, not her own, hoping he will become Prince Charming. Too late she discovers he is only charming, not sincere. Most abusive men are charming, but think the marriage license is a "license to hit."

A woman who stays in an abusive relationship believes that the man is superior and the head of the house. Sometimes steeped in fundamental religion, the couple accept their rigid stereotyped sex roles and strive at all costs to preserve the family. Instead of being in touch with her own feelings, the woman is trained how to intuit other people's emotions and how to meet their needs.

She becomes codependent, minimizes the abuser's violence, and denies what is happening in their home. When the violence starts, she uses the skills of mind reading to try and appease the abuser to avoid a beating. Sometimes, when the tension becomes too great, she may actually start an argument, "just to get it over with."

Abused women pay a heavy price for their attitude of selflessness. They learn the secret of survival is to appear cool and calm on the outside, even though their insides are shaking apart. The inner tension and fear they experience finds expression in numerous stress related diseases.

These self-sacrificing women show up in doctor's offices on a regular basis suffering from chronic headaches, chronic anxiety, panic attacks, backaches, stomach and digestive disorders, eczema, hives, high blood pressure, and other physical problems directly associated with repression of feelings—and the cuts, bruises, and broken bones they received "walking into a door." They develop Posttraumatic Stress Disorder, psychic numbing, depression, and the Battered Woman Syndrome. Many abused women eventually come to think escape is not possible: the only way out of the battering hell is to either be killed or kill the abuser.

Socialized in their role as wife, to please and serve their husband, when they get hit, they may think they did something wrong to deserve it. They often minimize, "It isn't that bad," or rationalize, "Dinner was late, I deserved to be slapped." They may deny anything wrong occurred, "You never saw your father push me down." "That never happened." She may use splitting, "He's a good provider." "He's a good father," to justify his behavior. Or, the battered wife may simply assess her situation and lack of economic resources, and choose to forget it. Both victims and their abusers are likely to minimize or deny the occurrence of spousal abuse. They may be unaware of the magnitude of the abuse, as the conditioning process is a gradual one. An abuser may begin by intimidation, such as verbal abuse, degrading the spouse, punching holes in walls with his fist, or by destroying or disposing of possessions owned by or valued by the partner.

The ups and downs in abusive relationships creates other psychological pathology as well. The abuse, and the times of peacefulness, or lack of battering, combine to create a traumatic bonding. This traumatic bonding is harder to break than steel— fused from love, resentment, pain and anger. Their fears connect like a lightening bolt, bonding the two in "addictive love." She can't let go. He can't let go. They think they can't live without each other.

As a woman is trained to be more assertive, she might be even more abused by her husband. When a woman tries to step outside the rigid stereotyped sex role to find herself, she might encounter the abusive use of power and control to put her back in "her place."

Chapter Seven

Men Who Batter

Not every male who was abused in childhood is a batterer, as is popularly believed. But men who batter usually witnessed abuse in their homes as they grew up. Witnessing or being a participant in violence in the family home is associated with later violence toward one's own partner. "I grew up watching my dad slap my mother around," said one batterer. "And he beat on me a few times, too."

In a study of more than 2,000 spouses, having observed hitting between one's parents was more strongly related to severe marital aggression than being hit as a teenager by one's parents, although both were factors (Kalmuss, 1984). This cycle of violence in which children observe, experience, and later inflict violence in their own adult relationships, is sometimes difficult to stop, as each generation tends to learn from the preceding one.

Other factors contributing to the escalation of abuse in relationships take into account the social models on television and in movies. The media is normalizing violence in our society.

David Knox, in his book, *Choices in Relationships: An Introduction to Marriage and the Family*, discusses the myriad of factors contributing to the rise in domestic violence, including the centuries-old custom of wife-beating, that for most of history enjoyed not only social acceptance, but legal protection. Western literature, the arts, and folk wisdom, all reflect that wife-beating was not only condoned, but encouraged. Ben Franklin's "Love well, whip well," and a 16th century English proverb, "A woman, an ass, and a walnut tree, bring the more fruit, the more beaten they be," reflect the easy acceptance of using force against one's wife. These notions about the appropriateness of violence within marriage remain deeply imbedded within our culture.

The law of reinforcement states that any behavior followed by a reward will increase the frequency of that behavior in the future. When spouses get their way as a result of violence, the odds increase that they will use violence in the future. "I've found that I can control my wife by beating her up now and then," one husband said. "She's due for another licking soon."

Sometimes violence has nothing to do with winning an argument or getting one's way. Rather, the abuser may feel frustrated due to job stress or bickering children. Any of these stressors can produce a feeling of anxious tension. The spouse may be blamed for the partner's unhappy, frustrated feelings, and beaten as a way of releasing that tension.

One abuser justified hitting his wife by saying, "Of course I hit her. She had dinner a half hour late." To their counselor's astonishment, his wife replied, "It was all my fault. The children were fighting, and I had to keep stopping them from hitting each other. I should have been paying more attention to what time it was so dinner could have been ready at six o'clock." His wife, like many battered women, believed it was her role to please and serve her husband. When abused, battered women often accept the blame and think they did something wrong.

Most battering is never recognized. "It is hard to know the exact figures since an estimated eighty percent of the cases of domestic violence alone, go unreported because battered women are ashamed, are mistakenly protecting their abusers, or are fearful of reprisals," says Jan Berliner Statman in her book, *The Battered Woman's Survival Guide.*

Many people think abusive men are antisocial, sadistic, thugs, unshaven, and wearing sloppy, dirty shirts and pants. Only ten percent are like this. Most of these men were sexually and physically abused in childhood and often end up in prison because they externalize and take their anger and rage out on society. Eighty percent of violent criminals have a child abuse history. Eighty-five to ninety percent of men on death row have severe child abuse in their history.

The other ninety percent of abusive men present a dual personality to the world. They are Dr. Jekyll at the job and Mr. Hyde when they go home. Often unusually charming and charismatic, no one would suspect them capable of battering their partners.

O.J. Simpson is a typical batterer. He was successful, well dressed, charming and well thought of. He battered his first wife.

Why was it so hard to believe he battered his second? As this book goes to press, the O.J. Simpson trial is still in progress.

In the book, *Shattered Dreams* (Dell Publishing, 1987), the wife of a prominent lawyer in the Reagan administration tells her true story. She endured physical and emotional abuse for seventeen years before she broke free. She urges women to speed up the process of leaving.

Most abusive men never change, even with treatment. Some counselors, having seen what continued abuse does to battered women, encourage them to leave, but also to take measures to insure their safety. Batterers are most dangerous when or after their partners leave. Three-fourths of women who are killed by their spouses are killed after they leave. If a woman is continually going back to her abuser, some counselors recommend that she may as well "just beat her head on the wall and save time." Staying with an abuser may lead to her death or being maimed for life.

Abusive men are found in all walks of life, in all neighborhoods, all races, all socioeconomic and financial levels, all educational levels; but most have a history of fundamental religion because that type of religion supports the philosophy of male dominance.

How do these men live with themselves? How can they say they are good people when they are beating and raping their wives and children? Through a combination of defense mechanisms, they deny, rationalize, split and forget that they have done any wrong. Battered women do the same thing when they make statements such as, "He's a good father." "He's not himself." "He didn't really mean it."

Batterers dehumanize women by seeing them as a piece of property. They then feel justified to do anything they want to them to get their way. An abuser may minimize or forget details, or the degree of injury, or rewrite history. Batterers depend on intimidating their victim, and they will do it whenever they can get away with it. Then they blame the victim for their violence. "She burned the coffee." After an abused woman hears enough times that the violence is her fault, she becomes brainwashed and believes it.

BRAIN INJURY

New research has shown sixty to seventy-five percent of batterers have frontal lobe head injuries. Head wounds happen when boys play football, have motorcycle accidents or fall out of a tree.

Fifty percent of batterers, abused in childhood, may have received brain damage when they were shook or hit. The head wound may not show up on a CAT scan, but usually can be detected through neuropsychological testing. Alcohol and drugs affect a person differently who has had a head wound. Frontal lobe injury reduces behavioral control and produces impulsive actions.

Many times, when a man is attacking a woman, he bangs her head into the wall. She may sustain a head wound. Head wounds cause people to lose control and react by attacking when they feel threatened. When men are killed during the course of domestic violence, it's usually the woman killing him in self-defense.

A person with a head wound regresses emotionally. Through retraining and time, they may regain their maturational development. But head wounds are no excuse for battering. These men don't blow up at work. They know they can't get away with it.

They can learn how to manage the condition, even if they don't know they have it. They beat their wives because it releases frustration, and they feel entitled to dominate and control women.

FEAR OF REJECTION

Batterers fear rejection. They fear rejection not only because of their own childhoods, but also because they believe the myth of male superiority. To be rejected by an "inferior woman" is unthinkable. They actually believe they must know all the answers, show strength, and never be afraid. Inwardly, they never feel adequate, or man enough. It is this deep seated fear of rejection and abandonment that spurs the jealousy and possessiveness, which drives the abuse. If a woman is controlled, she can't leave.

Many abusive men turn to alcohol or drugs to bolster and reinforce their sagging sense of manhood. Seventy-five to eighty percent of all battering involves the use of alcohol. Some turn to extramarital affairs to prove their masculinity. Secretly, batterers live in constant fear of being exposed for their own humanness. Full of shame (for not being man enough), abusive men often hide their fears behind a facade of false bravado.

Since abusive men do not credit women with any rights to make their own choices, they see other males as competitors and rivals. They think a woman can be taken from them by a stronger male. This primitive reasoning takes the form of the "bull in the pasture mentality."

Abusive men are jealous and possessive. To prevent fears of rejection and abandonment, they try and control where "their" woman goes, who she sees, and what she wears. A woman is viewed as a possession by an abusive man, and these men don't want to lose their possessions.

When fears of abandonment and rejection surface, these men may lose control—they push, shove, demean, humiliate, hit, and butcher. Much of battering behavior is a maneuver to live up to the false image of masculinity they think is real and to control the women they think they own.

COMMON CHARACTERISTICS

Both men and women in abusive relationships share characteristics
from their families of origin and their belief systems.

The Battered Woman	*The Batterer*
1. Low self-esteem	1. Low self-esteem
2. Believes the myths	2. Believes the myths
3. Strongly believes in the traditional family unit	3. Believes in male supremacy
4. Accepts responsibility for the batterer's actions	4. Blames others for his actions
5. Suffers from guilt, yet denies the terror and anger she feels. Attempts to control people and events in her environment to keep the batterer from losing his temper.	5. Exaggerated jealousy. In order for him to feel secure, he must become overinvolved in the woman's life. Suspicious of her relationships with others.
6. Presents a passive face to the world.	6. Presents a dual personality. (Dr. Jekyll and Mr. Hyde)
7. Has severe stress reactions with psychophysical complaints	7. Has severe stress reactions during which he uses drinking and wife beating to cope.
8. Uses sex as a way to establish intimacy	8. Frequently uses sex as an aggressive act of control
9. Believes that no one will be able to help her resolve her predicament except herself.	9. Does not believe his violent behavior should have consequences. Typically denies the problem; becomes enraged if the woman reveals the truth.

"Common characteristics" is copied by permission from Robert Geffner, Ph.D., Family Violence & Sexual Assault Institute, Tyler, Texas.

Even though sixty percent of women who are battered also recall sexual abuse in childhood, the single greatest risk to being battered is to be a female. The single greatest risk factor that makes a man a batterer is to come from a home where battering occurred, and he learned to role model that behavior (the gunpowder). A current explosive situation becomes the fuse. The batterer is often on drugs or alcohol when the fuse ignites the gunpowder, and the battering occurs.

The typical batterer is an angry man. He has a "me first" attitude. He is mostly concerned with taking care of his wants and needs of the moment. He "wants what he wants when he wants it." When he looks inside himself, nothing's there. He develops an *as if* personality to compensate for his inner emptiness. His chameleon type personality strives to become what others approve of outwardly, while inwardly he harbors life-long, deeply ingrained, malevolent, anti-social, criminal or manipulative attitudes and behaviors to get what he wants. He has no real reason to change because he feels no emotional pain for the injury he inflicts. Instead, he blames others for his problems.

VERBAL AND EMOTIONAL ABUSE

Violence has many faces. Verbal and emotional abuse occurs in one out of two marriages. These types of abuse always accompany and, in many cases, precede physical battering. Like hitting, targeted and repeated emotional abuse can have severe effects on the victim's sense of self and reality.

In some ways, the repeated humiliation of emotional and psychological abuse can be more damaging than physical abuse, and harder to overcome. Repeated verbal abuse results in brainwashing the victim into *learned helplessness*. Living under these conditions causes you to feel powerless, and question your sense of reality. It creates emotional instability and dependency. As a result, you may end up depressed, or make suicide attempts.

Consider what you would feel like if you were the target of:
- jokes about your habits/faults
- insults
- your feelings being ignored
- yelling, name calling
- repeated humiliation in public and in private
- labels such as "crazy," "bitch," "whore," "animal"
- put downs of your abilities as parent, worker, and lover
- threats to abuse the children or get custody of them
- insults to stay because you can't make it on your own

CYCLE OF VIOLENCE

The Cycle of Violence Theory, developed by Lenore Walker (1979) consists of three phases. During the initial phase, the abuser may verbally harass or make threats to his partner. Minor physical abuse may occur. Both the abuser and his partner/spouse try to control his behavior. Incidents are minimized or denied. Tension builds.

The emotional abuse starts out slowly, with little put downs. The abuser may first make a belittling remark. You hear "Bitch," underneath his breath. You think, that's only one time, he's upset. I won't say anything about it. I know he really doesn't mean it, and you think that's the end of it.

The next time it happens, you may let him know you're not happy about it. You're sure it will stop. But it doesn't. He adds, "fat slob" to the insult. You go on a diet. You invest energy thinking about it, hoping he'll change. He doesn't.

The insults escalate into psychological abuse. You're checked up on. Your expenses are questioned. You are prevented from working or going to school. You're not allowed to have money. He destroys your property; hurts the pets. He drives recklessly to frighten you, manipulates you with lies, or comes home drunk or high. He's jealous and possessive. He demands reports of where you've been and where you're going. He threatens to divorce you unless you comply. You hope he'll change.

During the second phase, the sexual abuse starts and the battering escalates to full fledged destructiveness.

Elements of marital sexual abuse:
- He may start having affairs.
- He acts angry or pouts if he is denied sex.
- He accuses you of affairs, and demands "whose baby is it?"
- He may rape you, hurt you sexually and judge your sexual performance, and/or refer to you as "a dry hole."
- He may say you're too fat.

You hope he'll change. You try harder.

The battering starts: *The abuse becomes uncontrollable.*
- You're pinned against a wall.
- You're held against your will.
- You're pushed, shoved, slapped; your arm is twisted.

Elements of major destructiveness and battering:
- He holds a gun or a knife on you.
- He bangs your head against a wall.
- He throws things at you.
- He bites and scratches you.
- He may stand or sit on you; kick or knee you.
- He may hit you in the stomach when you're pregnant.
- He threatens to kill you if you leave.

You believe him. The police may intervene.

Phase three is known as the honeymoon or loving respite. The batterer is remorseful and afraid of losing his partner. Apologies and promises are made about changes for the better. He may promise anything, beg forgiveness, buy gifts, and effusively communicative with a passion fueled by guilt.

He becomes, "the man I fell in love with." New hope surges in the calm and kindness when sexual interaction takes place. Many times, the honeymoon is simply a cessation of violence. The repentance is usually short-lived for the abuser. The ups and downs of the cycle of violence further cement the traumatic bonding.

EFFECTS OF VIOLENCE ON CHILDREN

Children who witness family violence are harmed just as much as if they are hit themselves. When children hear the screams and threats, when they see their father throwing their mother against walls, doors or onto the floor, when they see him pounding her with his fists until she bleeds, kicking her, choking her or cutting her, they are also victimized.

When they witness violence, children develop Posttraumatic Stress Disorder (nightmares, anxiety, fear and flashbacks), stomach aches and other psychosomatic symptoms, just the same as their mothers. Preschoolers often reenact the family violence in their play. Elementary school children may have school failure and develop sleep and eating disorders.

Children who grow up fearful do not mature normally. Their brain pathways and brain chemistry develop abnormally. The constant stress makes them hyper-vigilant, ready to run at a moment's notice. Unable to develop a *safe place* within, they feel insecure.

Children feel emotionally abandoned because their mother

99

is fighting for her own survival and cannot defend them. They are afraid they will lose both their mother and father. They feel powerless because they can't stop the violence. They don't understand why the people they love most are fighting.

In an effort to make sense out of what is going on, children reason it must be something they've done. They feel angry and wonder if their friend's fathers hit their mothers. They stop seeing their friends because they feel alone, isolated and different. They think it's only happening to them. Inwardly, they know something's wrong.

The children are afraid they may be hurt or lose someone they love. They're told not to talk about it. They're afraid others may find out. As the violence escalates, these children are also at risk for physical and sexual abuse.

In at least fifty to seventy percent of the homes where domestic violence occurs, the children are also physically and sexually abused. In fact, they have a fourteen times greater chance of being abused than in a nonviolent home. Research shows early suicide among six and seven year old children is due to abuse.

Adolescents commonly turn to drugs and alcohol to control or numb their thoughts and feelings. They often experience anxiety and depression. They have poor impulse control. Eighty percent of children who run away from home do so to escape the violence in the home and the sexual abuse perpetrated upon them.

These childhood victims continue to suffer from the consequences of the nightmare of violence, and carry their scars into adulthood. They grow up shy, unable to form close relationships or trust and love others. They are emotionally isolated, insecure, haunted by fear of abandonment, and suffer low self-esteem. They live their lives in quiet desperation, never disclosing the secrets of their distress.

In adulthood, they are unable to love themselves or others.

They do not feel compassion, empathy, care, or emotions of joy, generosity, or genuine happiness for another's success and well-being. Their relationships are like empty shells, devoid of real love and affection. Even when these adults act *as if* they are loving, you know it's just not real.

ABUSE IDENTIFICATION QUESTIONNAIRE

Read over the Abuse Identification Questionnaire and answer the questions honestly. If you have a question as to whether you have been abused, the questionnaire can help.

__ Have you changed locations or residences frequently?
__ Are either you or your spouse extremely religious?
__ Were either you or your spouse physically abused in childhood?
__ Were either of you sexually abused during childhood?
__ Was there a history of violence in either of your families?
__ If so, was the violence directed at the children?
__ Was the violence directed at one parent by the other?
__ Did either your spouse or your parents abuse alcohol?
__ Does your spouse treat his parents roughly or disrespectfully?
__ Has your spouse ever hit his parents, brothers, or sisters?
__ Has your spouse ever threatened to harm you?
__ Are your spouse's problems usually blamed on you or others?
__ Have you been attacked or blamed when your spouse got angry?
__ Are you afraid of your spouse's temper?
__ When drinking, does your spouse get rough or violent?
__ Has your spouse ever deliberately hurt you?
__ Did your spouse ever hit a former spouse or lover?
__ Has your spouse ever deliberately hurt or killed a pet?

*used with the permission of the Family Violence & Sexual Assault Institute, Tyler, Texas

__ Does your spouse have a Dr. Jekyll and Mr. Hyde personality?
__ Do you usually give in to settle arguments?
__ Are your children afraid when your spouse is angry?
__ Do the children have emotional or school problems?
__ Do the children display extremes in behavior?
__ Does any child assume a parental role in the family by waiting on you or caring for younger siblings?
__ Have you felt free to invite family or friends to visit you?
__ Are you socially isolated?
__ Does your spouse insist on going everywhere with you?
__ Is your spouse suspicious of your every move?
__ Is your spouse an extremely jealous person?
__ Has you spouse accused you of having an affair? Have you?
__ Has your spouse ever forced you to have sex even though you did not want to?
__ Have you ever called, or thought of calling, the police because an argument was getting out of control?
__ Have your neighbors or friends ever called the police?
__ If the police were called, was your spouse arrested or given a citation?
__ Does your spouse ever threaten to take the children where you could not find them? Did this ever occur?

If you answered yes to most of the above questions, turn to the Appendix and fill out the Danger Assessment. You need to seek counseling and do something about your situation. Where there is severe battering, there is a danger of homicide.

Domestic violence is a dark subject about the dark side of people; a side most would rather not acknowledge. Nicole Simpson had a Constitutional and human right not to live in fear. So does every woman. Women's rights are human rights. Amnesty International fights for human rights for nameless males in foreign countries when the woman living right next door could be living in terror and is beaten to death in her own home.

It's women in the last twenty-five years who have said, "enough." It's women who have established the safe houses, domestic violence intervention services, rape crisis services, child physical and sexual abuse programs, and self-defense courses. These programs were started out of desperation. They are, however, only a Band-Aid to the real problem: violence. Women alone can't prevent violence.

Males must assist in stopping male violence against women. Until men say to other males that violence is unacceptable, and more than that, there will be zero tolerance for gender violence in this country, it will go on. Until severe penalties are set, and the law is consistently enforced whether women prosecute or not, until men are prepared to help change society, the violence will go on.

Women can't do it alone. We need the help of decent males who find violence against women as abhorrent as we do. Until the majority of males develop the social conscience and political will to stop it, the violence will continue.

VICTIM NO MORE

Chapter Eight

Alternatives To
Spouse/Partner Violence

Violence has become a way of life by the time many couples come for counseling. Often, it is too late in the relationship to do any good as years and years of violence leads to incredible anger on the part of the bitter, battered, spouse—anger and resentment that is almost impossible to go beyond.

She's furious because of all the years of intimidation. Once she feels safe, she won't stop telling the abuser just how mad she is at him. It is very hard to put the past in the past because of all the old hurts and wounds. But a relationship based on pain cannot grow. Working through the resentment and anger is hard work for the battered spouse and needs to be done with the help of a therapist trained in domestic violence.

In order for counseling to be effective, it is important that the batterer assume one hundred percent of the responsibility for *his own behavior*. It is not society's responsibility, and it is not the therapist's. Blaming and threatening the partner is unacceptable.

Batterers have the ability to stop their violent behavior, even brain damaged batterers. They can learn to avoid the situations that set them off and learn to raise their frustration tolerance level. They don't hit their bosses, and they can choose not to hit their wives.

An experiment in Minneapolis showed that if the violent person in a family disturbance is arrested and removed from the home, even for a few hours, the chances of future family violence are dramatically decreased (Rosellini & Worden, 1985).

Counseling the marital partners together is not recommended for people with a diagnosis of sociopathic or paranoid personality, or even those who are excessively jealous. It is best if partners are first interviewed separately due to the intimidation and control that has occurred during the relationship.

The battered woman may not feel free to talk openly if her abusive partner is present. She may still feel as though she's walking on eggshells when he's around. In addition, before interviewing any couple, an assessment needs to be made about whether the batterer will use information obtained during counseling to further control, put down, humiliate or emotionally blackmail the spouse.

It is important that the following preconditions are in effect in order for counseling with couples to take place.

- The abused woman and perpetrator both desire this type of treatment.
- The abused woman has a safety plan and understands the potential dangers.
- An adult must accept responsibility if child abuse has occurred.
- There are no custody issues if a divorce is in process.
- There is a low probability of danger.
- The perpetrator does not harbor obsessional ideas toward the abused woman.
- Therapists are trained in both family therapy and domestic violence.
- The use of alcohol or drugs during treatment is prohibited. Seventy-five to eighty percent of battering involves the use of alcohol or drugs.
- If there has been substance abuse, then treatment for this is required.
- Neither partner exhibits psychotic behavior.
- It is unnecessary for the partners to live together for them to benefit from counseling. In fact, if violence has escalated, it is wise if the partners only see each other during the counseling hour, at first.

Even though there is very little fun and humor in a relationship where battering has occurred, both partners still have a great deal invested in the relationship and are afraid of loss. This threat of loss is the batterer's motivation to change. If the couple doesn't have a basic foundation of love and commitment, marriage counseling won't work. If this is lacking, they are better off to mediate a divorce.

When they first start therapy, both partners need to agree that there will be no arguments. They can wait to discuss their differences when the counselor is present. If the wife is battered during the time they are in treatment, she must file charges at the police department. The batterer must suffer the legal consequences. In fact, if battering occurs during treatment, this may be the only way he can learn *violence is unacceptable*. If he is able to batter and have his way without suffering the consequences, he is actually being rewarded. You can be sure behavior that is rewarded will continue.

People who have been in abusive relationships often don't know what or how they feel. They're "numbed out." Learning to identify and express feelings is very important. In my book, *Panic No More, Your Guide to Overcome Panic Attacks*, you will find specific chapters on how to learn to identify and express feelings.

DEALING WITH ANGER

Anger, like all other emotions, is neither good nor bad. You simply feel what you feel. It's your response to it that makes it positive or negative. Hitting, choking, or breaking things are not appropriate expressions of anger. Learn to recognize bodily changes as anger approaches. Indicators of oncoming anger include the heart speeding up, glands sweating, face turning red, and the clenching of the fist or jaw. When you first learn to recognize and deal with anger, take thirty minutes out to be alone as you experience anger approaching. This may help you avoid losing control.

"Anger Eaters" help defuse angry emotions. "Anger Eaters" are cards on which to write: (a) the incident that made you angry; (b) how you responded to the situation; and (c) how you would prefer to handle it.

The process of writing helps integrate and defuse anger. The cards also become references to evaluate your anger coping patterns, and the progress you are making in instilling new ways of dealing with it. "Anger Eaters" teach you how to think through anger instead of simply reacting in a knee jerk fashion.

Jogging or walking briskly is also good for anger or stress reduction. A walk around the block can help clear your mind. Other time-out activities include listening to music, sitting quietly or peaceful daydreaming. If explosive anger where hitting others has been a problem for you, punching a bag is not a good outlet. Hitting may remind you of striking people or encourage the destruction of unacceptable objects.

Everyone needs a room of her own where she can go to be away from everything for a while. If you feel tense, just go to that room for long enough to relax. Another method for relieving tenseness is to stop for a minute and take some deep breaths. This adds oxygen to the body and helps you think more clearly. It helps you to calm down, and shift the focus away from the stressful situation. Talking about the stressful situation to another person is also helpful. Awareness of the physical symptoms that proceed anger and then "talking it out" with a trusted person may alleviate "blowing-up" and also help reduce stress.

Relaxation exercises calm you down and let you decide how to handle your anger and reduce stress and frustration. The simplest of these exercises is to tell your various body parts to relax and be calm and quiet.

Meditation is another way to calm down from anger. There are several meditation procedures given in *Panic No More, Your Guide to Overcome Panic Attacks*. One of the easiest ways to calm yourself is "breath counting." Count "one" for the first breath, "two" for the second breath, "three" for the third breath, and "four" for the fourth breath. Then start back at one and continue doing this for ten minutes. Breath counting requires a great deal of concentration, but produces excellent results.

Mental imagery is another excellent way to manage stress and anger. Think of a very peaceful, soothing, and relaxing scene. For example, picture a peaceful blue sky, or a lovely green meadow. While focusing on this, breathe slowly and naturally. These images help clear the mind.

When your counselor gives the go-ahead to discuss conflicts outside of the therapy hour (when you are back in control of your angry feelings and do not act them out), follow the fair fighting rules listed below to discuss areas of conflict with your partner. You might also make up a list of dirty fighting rules you have been using as a couple, just as a reminder of what not to do. Many couples get a big laugh out of doing this.

Fair Fighting Rules:
1. Agree on what you are going to discuss, and write the topic down. Be simple and direct. State *specifically* what you are angry about in plain language. "I am angry about ___."
2. Stay in the present; within the last forty-eight hours. Don't drag up old problems or argue about details.
3. Be assertive (self-valuing) rather than aggressive (getting the other person whatever it takes). Avoid lecturing, finger pointing, blaming, (it's all your fault) judging, labeling (you are bad), and score keeping (two years ago you ___).
4. Stay with "I" messages. "I think, " "I feel," or "In my opinion."
5. Use active listening. Repeat to the other person what you heard them say. "What I heard you say is _____." Get their agreement about what you heard them say before responding.
6. Do not try to make someone "wrong" so you can be "right."
7. Fight about one thing at a time. Unless you are being abused,

hang in there. Go for a solution rather than being right. After you express your anger, release it.

The flip side of anger is helplessness. Some abusers, when they feel helpless, go into a rage in order to trigger their endorphins (like a runner's high). An endorphin "rush" makes them feel strong and powerful.

Someone who has been abused in childhood often has an unconscious scanner searching for those he can control. When your behavior and posture emulate victim consciousness, you may trigger the response of intimidation in the controller. Body posture, assertiveness, and self-esteem are all interconnected. How you stand, walk, and talk, all give off nonverbal messages. Victim-type nonverbal messages, remind the abuser of his own vulnerability and fears of helplessness and powerlessness from his childhood.

When the controller senses victim consciousness, he may overreact by assuming a *power over* position. He may then do whatever he can get away with, and often that is what was done to him. After he has intimidated someone else, he feels calm because his abusive act releases his own fear and tension. He can relax because the abuse has happened to someone else, not him.

Insecurity, jealousy and rage stem from childhood. Both the controller and his partner fear abandonment. They think no one else would want them because they feel so worthless. As the years pass, the fear of loss escalates the violence. The abuse eventually causes the partner to leave in a self-fulfilling prophecy.

It cannot be stated enough: the controller sees his partner as a piece of property he owns. He thinks other men will try and steal her (his property). At the bottom of his irrational self-talk are feelings of worthlessness. He may think, "If I'm not tough, she'll think I'm weak." "I need to show her I'm in control." "If she

talks to another man, it means she wants to go to bed with him."
After thinking a few of these thoughts, an explosive outburst
may occur.

Faulty self-talk takes the form of:

1. Black & white thinking. This is the tendency to see things
   in an all-or-nothing fashion. You can also recognize this
   type of thinking by words such as "never," "always,"
   "nothing," and "everyone," appearing in the sentence.
   "You're either for me or against me." "Nothing ever works
   out for me."
2. Minimizing. This is the tendency to down play events. "It
   was only a little slap." "He really didn't mean it."
3. Mind-reading. This is the tendency to assume you know
   something without checking it out. Remember, assume is
   spelled ass-u-me. In other words, to *assume* is to make an
   ass out of you and me. "My husband didn't call today . . . he
   must not care about me." "She's looking at that man. She
   must want him."
4. Awfulizing. The prediction that things will turn out "awful"
   for you. "I'm not going to make it through counseling."
5. Blaming. The tendency to unfairly blame yourself or others.
   "It's all my fault," or "You always mess everything up for
   me."
6. Down-putting. The tendency to put yourself down for
   having a problem or making a mistake. "I'm in counseling,
   I must be crazy."
7. Emotional reasoning. The tendency to conclude that if you
   feel a certain way about yourself, then it must be true. "I
   feel rejected. Everybody must be rejecting me." "Since I
   feel guilty, I must have done something wrong."

Faulty self-talk comes from irrational beliefs originating in childhood, and not about what is going on at the present time. When you do faulty-self talk, you are creating reasons to explain why you feel the way you do. This is called emotional reasoning. You are not examining the source of the discomfort.

One man, who had been away on a long business trip, found that as he drove closer and closer to his home, he began feeling tense. As the tension increased, he imagined his wife having an affair. He then decided that was what caused his tension.

When he got home, he yelled and screamed at his wife, and threatened to beat her up. By this time, there was nothing she could do that would convince him she wasn't having an affair. Emotional reasoning can be dangerous.

The ability to change faulty self-talk begins with recognizing when you are doing it. Examples of self-faulty talk* and how to correct it are listed below. Look it over and see if anything listed fits you.

For Women

Category	Faulty Self-Talk	Positive Self-Talk
Fear and Anxiety	I'm afraid I will always be alone.	I can have close relationships and I can depend upon myself— whether or not I stay in this relationship.
Anger and Frustration	I hate my spouse - I want to hurt him.	My spouse is responsible for the abuse, and my anger is a normal response.
Guilt and Remorse	I am responsible for the abuse - I caused it.	My partner is responsible for the abuse. I was a victim.

*adapted from the Family Violence and Sexual Assault Institute, Tyler, TX

Category	Faulty Self-Talk	Positive Self-Talk
Shame & Self-Disgust	I will always be helpless.	I need not be a victim.
Sadness	I am empty. I have no hope. I am suicidal.	I am whole and I can be happy. It is up to me.

For Men

Category	Faulty Self-Talk	Positive Self-Talk
Fear and Anxiety	If I don't control her she will leave me.	She is a free person. She is more likely to stay if I do not try to control her.
Anger and Frustration	I don't mean to hurt her, but she makes me do it.	I am in control of myself and I take full responsibility for my behavior.
Guilt and Remorse	She makes me hurt her and then I feel bad.	When I control my actions, I feel good about myself.
Shame & Self-Disgust	I am not confident in myself. I cannot trust anyone.	I feel confident in some areas of my life. myself. I can trust some people.
Sadness	I am sad. I want to die.	I can change. I can be happy. It is up to me.

Practice staying on an adult level when communicating. It is an adult response to learn to "agree to disagree." A compromise seeks outcomes where both parties get something out of it, instead of one winning and the other losing.

Throughout their lives, controllers have only learned that losing power means helplessness. This fear of helplessness has led to all-or-nothing thinking. Controllers think the only way to avoid fears of helplessness is to take power before they are abused. Unfortunately, that eventually causes the very reaction they fear most—abandonment. No one likes to be controlled, intimidated, and battered. Sooner or later, the victim will make good her escape.

The one way to insure the relationship will survive is to learn how to treat each other with dignity and respect. People don't agree on everything, or like the same things. An opinion is simply an opinion, nothing more. Allow others the separateness and individuation they require to become mature individuals.

If you believe that you are being frustrated, annoyed, insulted, or attacked, and feel angry, don't respond immediately. Learn to control yourself before you react. Take several short, deep, breaths to fill your chest, and relax as you breathe out. Think of other possible explanations for what is making you angry. Think through the consequences of your behavior and the different ways you can react. Respond in some way that will control your anger. Find an alternative to aggression.

As you prepare for a stressful situation, repeat the following statements to yourself. "This could be a rough situation, but I know how to deal with it." "I can work out a plan to handle this." "Easy does it." "Remember, stick to the issues and don't take it personally." "There won't be any need for an argument."

As the situation materializes, repeating the following statements to yourself can help calm you enough to think clearly. "As long as I keep my cool, I'm in control of the situation." "I don't need to prove myself." "Don't make more of this than absolutely necessary." "Getting angry means losing control. Instead, think of what I have to do." "Look for the positives and do not jump to conclusions."

If your muscles are getting tight, take a deep breath, and relax. Allow things to slow down. Say, "Remember to take the issue point by point." "Anger is a signal of what I need to do." "Time for problem solving." "Even if the other party wants me to get angry, I am going to deal with it constructively."

Once the situation is over, remind yourself, "I handled that one pretty well." "My pride can get me into trouble." "I am doing better at this all the time." "I can actually get through this without blowing up." Remember, the one who gets angry gives up control. It is important to relate on an adult level, and not trigger the helplessness or powerlessness of the inner child who may quickly turn those fears into rage.

Once the violence has stopped, and the anger is under control, it's time to work on changing attitudes. Rigid sex stereotyped roles are easiest to challenge with role reversal. For example, the woman can make the sexual advances, ask the man out on a date, pay the bill, and do the driving. It's fun to experiment in these ways.

Another way to equalize and neutralize power is to get on the same level. If your partner is taller than you, stand on a chair so you can be taller for a change. Practice communicating from this vantage point, and see how it makes you feel. In the animal kingdom, as well as in ancient cultures, power and dominance are based on positions of height. Remember the stories where no one's head could be higher than the King's head? A primitive sense of power and dominance, based on height, may be coded in our brains.

Changing attitudes changes feelings. Stop the cycle of violence before it is passed on to the next generation. By being assertive, you learn how to meet your needs without stepping on someone else. Once you respect another person for themselves— not as a piece of property—you can truly love and have empathy for others. You will not harm someone you love.

Chapter Nine

Sexual Harassment

Mary Beth was sexually harassed by the psychiatric resident on the mental health unit. He was the team leader and over Mary Beth in terms of authority. She was a student intern. Soon after her internship started, he called her into his office, presumably to discuss a patient, but proceeded, instead, to chase her around his desk.

Afterwards, he accosted her in the hospital hall whenever he saw her, drove by her house and telephoned her at all hours of the day and night. He pleaded for her to marry him (he was already married and had four children), and talked about the unpleasant details in his marriage. Mary Beth asked him to stop.

When nothing she did or said seemed to deter him from the unwanted and repeated advances, Mary Beth became stressed. She talked the situation over with a coworker. The advice given was to go to her superior and let him handle the problem for her. She did.

Mary Beth's superior went to the resident and told him to leave her alone. The resident refused, saying, "She's under my authority and you can't tell me what to do." The psychiatric resident and Mary Beth's superior then argued over who had dominion over her. These two professionals decided to settle the dispute with a fist fight in the hospital parking lot, as if they were adolescent school boys.

About that time, the Mental Health Director arrived and broke up the fight. After he learned what had happened, he transferred the psychiatric resident to another unit in the hospital, and gave Mary Beth's superior a verbal thrashing.

That was the end of the harassment, except for a few telephone calls over the next fifteen years. The resident (now a psychiatrist), would telephone Mary Beth to say he had obtained a divorce, and would she please see him. "No," she answered, and hung up.

He called after every divorce. Four times in all, and once threatened suicide if she wouldn't be with him. She told him that she would loan him her gun if he needed it. That was the end of the harassment. After that, she heard he had lost his medical license for having intercourse with a patient in a hospital seclusion room. Apparently, he never did learn appropriate boundaries.

Ruth, a psychologist, was also employed at a prestigious psychiatric hospital. Her boss, the Clinical Director of the hospital, decided he wanted her to sit in on his therapy sessions and interviews with patients and fellow professionals, and follow him as he made rounds. He called her into his office for extended, unnecessary conversations. He made references to having sex with an artificial prosthesis. In general, he was "overly friendly," and "handsy," which made her feel uncomfortable and unable to concentrate on her work. She was preoccupied with trying to avoid getting trapped where he could brush up against her.

Ruth discussed this problem with her psychology supervisor, who told her there was nothing she could do. Ruth then went to the Medical Director, and mentioned the problem to him. "The doctor's happily married. I don't think anyone would believe you. If you file a complaint, he'll fire you. Better forget it. Besides, there isn't anything anyone can do about it because of the Clinical Director's position of power over the rest of the staff," the Medical Director warned.

Ruth told the harassing Clinical Director that clinical sessions with her patients were private and he couldn't sit in, and that her schedule was too busy for her to sit in on his. She avoided him whenever she could.

The Clinical Director retaliated. He took away Ruth's office and all her clinical work. She was no longer allowed to see patients for counseling or group therapy. Ruth was assigned to an inpatient unit where she had to clock in and out and was only allowed to do menial tasks not in her job description.

In team meetings, the Clinical Director either ignored what she said, directly contradicted her, or in some way ridiculed her. He refused her vacation requests and professional leave to attend conferences and seminars. He ostracized Ruth by intimidating other professionals into not having anything to do with her.

Finally, Ruth requested sick leave because of health reasons. The Clinical Director accused her of deserting her post. Ruth had called in every day and even had a doctor's statement attesting to her illness. The Clinical Director said he never received her messages.

Fortunately, Ruth found the carbon copies of the telephone messages and the signatures of who took them. When she approached the secretary and asked her to verify the calls to the Personnel Director, the secretary said she was afraid she would lose her job if she did.

When Ruth was called in to talk to the Personnel Director at the Clinical Director's request (to be fired), the Personnel Director said he knew that the Clinical Director was lying because he had called him to get her telephone number. The Clinical Director had sent it to him on the message slip he said he never received.

Ruth showed the Personnel Director documentation of the harassment she had been subjected to over the past months. She also showed him recommendations attesting to her competency from fellow professionals who could not be intimidated by the Clinical Director. The Personnel Director refused to fire her, but also said there was nothing he could do about the harassment because of the Clinical Director's power.

Ruth did not want to quit her job as it would look bad on her resume and might cause her a problem getting other employment. She also thought, as a psychologist, she should be able to handle the situation. She thought the Clinical Director was very ill. She was able to confirm that indeed, he did have multiple problems, such as advanced diabetes, heart disease, and hardening of the arteries.

Ruth thought if she could put up with it long enough, the Clinical Director would eventually leave or die. Tolerating an intolerable situation, Ruth began to suffer numerous stress related problems. Her hair fell out by the fist full. She developed aches and pains; headaches and sleeping problems. Finally, she quit, losing her retirement, benefits, and income. She knew her health was more important. The Clinical Director left nine months later for a position in another state.

THE PROBLEM OF SEXUAL HARASSMENT

Sexual harassment is endemic. The problem of sexual harassment, as well as sexual victimization and violence against women, is about male privilege, power, control, and dominance. It is about the subjugation, suppression, submission, disrespect and disregard of women in an attempt to "keep them in their place." It is perpetuated in a paternalistic society by the myth of male superiority. Thanks to Clarence Thomas and Anita Hill, the subject of sexual harassment is out in the open.

Almost every woman has her own story of sexual harassment. It happens to all kinds of women, in all types of jobs, at every level of the working world. Studies show that as many as eighty-eight percent of working women and fifteen percent of working men have experienced sexual harassment. It is a serious problem in the United States and many other countries.

In our schools, a 1993 study entitled "Hostile Hallways," showed that eighty-one percent of the girls and almost as many boys reported being sexually harassed. Types of harassment reported by the students included jokes, sexual comments, sexy looks, being grabbled or touched, flashed, intentionally brushed up against in a sexual way, or mooned.

"The impact on girls is far more devastating," says Mary Llewellyn Parker, Oklahoma psychologist, "perhaps because girls lose self-esteem as they enter the middle school years (from age twelve on). Girls often lose their sense of self by relinquishing their own interests and activities in an effort to sustain relationships with others, particularly with boys. They then began to define their worth in terms of their relationships as well as how they are perceived by others."

Almost five times as many girls as boys (thirty-nine percent compared with eight percent) who have been harassed, say they're afraid in school. Furthermore, forty-three percent of harassed girls feel less confident about themselves, as compared with fourteen percent of boys (Webb, 1994). The harassment our children face at school is merely a reflection of our culture. Parents that talk to their children about how to deal with sexual harassment before they're confronted with it, will have a better chance.

Students at academic institutions are protected from sexual harassment by Title IX of the 1972 Education Amendments. Title IX is administered by the Office for Civil Rights, which defines sexual harassment as "verbal or physical conduct of a sexual nature, imposed on the basis of sex, by an employee or recipient (of an institution receiving federal funds) that denies, limits, provides different, or conditions the provision of aid, benefits, services, or treatment protected under Title IX."

Sexual harassment generally does not happen to you because of the way you dress, talk, or behave. In fact, sexual harassment isn't necessarily about sex—it's about power. When someone at work uses sexual behavior to control you—whether it's to force you to have sex or just to make you feel uncomfortable—that's sexual harassment.

Conduct that might be harmless or even enjoyable in a social situation, can be upsetting at work. Sexual behavior that is repeated, unwanted, and interferes with your job has crossed the line; it is not only inappropriate, it is illegal. When the other person's behavior is having a negative effect on your work life, it is sexual harassment.

Sexual harassment covers a wide range of behaviors, from obvious acts, such as fondling, to subtle ones such as making suggestive remarks. In general, sexual harassment is any behavior in the workplace that:
- relates to your gender or sexuality
- is intentional and/or repeated
- is unwanted and not returned
- interferes with your ability to do your job

It is also any behavior in the workplace where:
- it is stated or understood that you must submit to the behavior in order to get or keep a job
- employment decisions and job status are based on whether or not you go along with the behavior
- the behavior creates an offensive work atmosphere

For example, if a co-worker accidentally brushes against you, it should not be considered sexual harassment. However, if that person repeatedly finds opportunities to brush against you, it is no longer accidental—it is deliberate. Behavior like this, which may make you feel uncomfortable and adversely affect your work, is sexual harassment.

It most often occurs between an older man in a superior position and a younger woman in an inferior position. Harassment is more likely to occur in jobs in the lower staff levels and also in workplaces where males are in the majority. Eighty percent of all working women are still clustered in eighty of the four hundred ten job classifications listed by the U.S. Department of Labor.

Many secretaries, waitresses, and assistants deal with harassment daily. Divorced and single women are more prone for harassment. A single or divorced woman is considered "fair game." Married or widowed women tend to be respected as other men's property. But, a woman's marital status, however chaste, does not render her immune from harassment.

Sexual harassment is a costly hazard for women, for the workplace, and for the culture. It victimizes women of all ages, races, classes, work experiences, backgrounds, and sexual orientations. The common assumption that sexual harassment of women is harmless, trivial, or easy for women to handle, is wrong. Many women are in denial about how serious a problem it is. They may think, "He really didn't mean it." "It wasn't that bad." Denial allows the victim to avoid dealing with the problem. But the comments, jokes, and innuendoes mount up and can destroy confidence and undermine self-esteem.

THE FACTS ABOUT SEXUAL HARASSMENT*

- Sexual harassment is the inappropriate sexualizing of an otherwise nonsexual relationship, an assertion by men of the primacy of a woman's sexuality over her role as a worker or professional colleague or student (Fitzgerald and Ormerod, 1991a).
- Sexual harassment is about power, not sex.
- Sexual harassment is sexual victimization, a form of sex discrimination, not "boys will be boys."
- Sexual harassment is part of the continuum of violence against women.
- Fifty to eighty-five percent of American women will experience some form of sexual harassment during their academic or working life (Hughes and Sandler, 1986, 1988; U.S. Merit Systems Protection Board 1987).
- Two out of three women in the military have been sexually harassed. (The New York Times, September 12, 1991).
- In the typical sexual harassment case, the accuser becomes

*adapted from *Sexual Harassment: Research & Resources*, a report prepared by The National Council for Research on Women

the accused, and the victim is twice-victimized.

- Women are nine times more likely than men to quit a job because of sexual harassment, five times more likely to transfer, and three times more likely to lose jobs (Konrad and Gutek, 1986).

- Most women who are sexually harassed never say anything. They are afraid they would be blamed (victim blaming); they fear retaliation; they do not believe anything will come of it; or they have concern for the harasser. They didn't want to hurt him.

- Ninety percent of the Fortune 500 companies surveyed have received sexual harassment complaints; over a third had been hit with law suits; nearly a fourth had been repeatedly sued. Sexual harassment costs a typical Fortune 500 company $6.7 million per year—a cost of $282.53 per employee.

- Meaningful preventive steps can be taken by a company for $200,000—a cost of $8.41 per employee. It is thirty-four times more expensive to ignore the problem (Klein, 1988).

- Men use sexual harassment as a way of objecting to women's presence on the job and keeping them "in their place" when they have to work with them (Moccio, 1991).

- There are no typical harassers. Most are older than their victims (but some are younger), married (but some are single), and of the same race as their victims. Some harass many women, others harass only once (Fitzgerald, 1991b).

The Sexual Harassment Trauma Syndrome

The effects of stress as a result of sexual harassment are tremendous and can eventually lead to the Sexual Harassment Trauma Syndrome. This syndrome negatively affects the emotional and physical well being, and causes changes in career, self-perception, social and sexual abilities.

The emotional reactions include: anxiety, shock, denial, Posttraumatic Stress Disorder, fear, anger, frustration, insecurity, betrayal, embarrassment, confusion, self-consciousness, shame, powerlessness, guilt, isolation, depression, self-questioning, loss of confidence, and self-blame.

Physical reactions include: headaches, hair loss, sleep disturbance, lethargy, gastrointestinal distress, nausea, crying spells, hypervigilance, dermatological reactions, weight fluctuations, nightmares, phobias, panic reactions, genitourinary distress, respiratory problems, and substance abuse.

Eventually there are changes in self-perception such as: negative self-concepts/self-esteem, lack of competency, lack of control, isolation, hopelessness, and powerlessness.

The social, interpersonal relatedness and sexual effects include: withdrawal, fear of new people or situations, lack of trust, lack of focus, self-preoccupation, changes in social network patterns, negative attitudes and behavior in sexual relationships, potential sexual disorders associated with stress and trauma, and changes in dress or physical appearance.

The career patterns that are negatively affected include: changes in study and work habits, loss of job or performance, unfavorable performance evaluations, drop in academic or work performance because of stress, lower grades as punishment for reporting sexual harassment or for noncompliance with sexual advances, absenteeism, withdrawal from work and school, and changes in career goals.

Sexual Harassment Laws

There are four types of laws that can apply to sexual harassment in the workplace: equal employment opportunity; labor; tort; and criminal. The United States sexual harassment laws and policies are gender-neutral, but it is mainly women who suffer from this crime. Under Title VII of the 1964 Civil Rights Act, sexual harassment is unlawful as a form of sexual discrimination.

The effect of this Act was minimal until 1986 when the Supreme Court established that sexual harassment, including a hostile work environment, was a violation of civil rights, even if the victim suffers no economic loss. For sexual harassment to be actionable it must be sufficiently severe or pervasive to "alter the conditions of the victim's employment and create an abusive working environment."

The Supreme Court's key opinions were:
- Sexual harassment is a form of sex discrimination, illegal under Title VII of the 1964 Civil Rights Act.
- Sexual harassment is illegal even if the victim suffered only a hostile work environment and not the loss of economic or tangible job benefits.
- Employers are not automatically liable for sexual harassment by their supervisors.
- Lack of knowledge of the harassment does not automatically relieve the employer of liability for the supervisors' harassment.
- The complainant's consent to the behavior does not relieve the employer of liability. The question is not the "voluntariness" of the complainant's participation, but if her conduct indicated that the behavior was unwelcome.
- The complainant's behavior, such as provocative speech and dress, may be considered in determining whether the complainant found particular sexual advances unwelcome.

Types of Sexual Harassment Claims
There are two types of sexual harassment claims. The first is

called *quid pro quo* (this for that). It is where a condition of employment, like keeping a job or getting a raise, is openly or implicitly offered in exchange for sexual favors. If you don't comply with the advances, retaliatory action may be threatened.

In a *quid pro quo* situation, the sexual behavior does not have to be physical. For example, a supervisor might give the best work assignments to employees who flirt with him. This is illegal sexual harassment even if the "trade" is merely understood and never stated outright. The second type of harassment, called *hostile environment*, is defined as unwelcome and demeaning sexual behavior that creates an intimidating, hostile and offensive work atmosphere for any employee.

The employee who repeatedly makes sexual jokes or innuendos in front of a colleague, even though he knows she doesn't like it, is sexually harassing her by creating a hostile environment. So is the employee who keeps finding excuses to brush against a co-worker. Most claims for sexual harassment involve a *hostile environment.*

When sexual harassment takes place, the offender is not the only one at fault. It is the legal obligation of every employer to provide a workplace that is free from sexual harassment. This responsibility is spelled out by the Equal Employment Opportunity Commission (EEOC) in their Guidelines on Discrimination Because of Sex.

The Equal Employment Opportunity Commission defines sexual harassment as unwanted sexual advances, requests for sexual favors, or other verbal or physical conduct of a sexual nature. Included in the definition is deliberate, repeated, unwelcome sexual pressure, and behavior that one is not in a position to refuse. Sexual harassment can be devastating to the victim and to the employer.

The settlements made by the courts are reflecting that this

injustice is now being taken seriously. The Civil Rights Act of 1991 amends Title VII and allows victims to recover awards for compensatory and punitive damages in cases of sexual harassment. The monetary amounts of awards are based on the number of employees working for the company: $50,000 for companies of 100 or less employees, $100,000 for companies of 200 or fewer employees, $200,000 for companies of 500 or less employees, and $300,000 for companies of over 500 employees.

Many victims of sexual harassment still do not file charges because they fear reprisal or loss of privacy. But in 1993, nearly twelve thousand sexual harassment complaints—almost double the number of those in 1990—were filed at the Equal Employment Opportunity Commission. Experts say that during the next five years, as this type of crime receives more attention, more legal action will be filed resulting in billions of dollars in settlements.

SEXUAL HARASSMENT POLICIES

Almost all large organizations now have policies regarding sexual harassment. Sexual harassment training programs are generally viewed as "preventative maintenance" by employers. Recent judicial decisions and, in some states, legislative developments, are forcing employers to develop and implement plans to eliminate sexual harassment in the workplace.

Employers may avoid costly litigation and liability if they can show they did everything possible to avert the sexual harassment. Support of top level management is very important in stopping sexual harassment.

Post sexual harassment policies where they can be read by every employee. Training and education are also important parts of a total sexual harassment policy. Be sure to make clear to everyone that sexual harassment will not be tolerated.

TEN MISTAKES MANAGERS MAKE

- Denying that a problem exists.
- Resisting change, because they think they are doing everything that is required of them.
- Labeling a woman within the organization as motherly, a sex object or a militant feminist.
- Thinking women shouldn't have power.
- Refusing to grant to women the same leadership opportunities as men.
- Misunderstanding what constitutes sexual harassment.
- Tolerating pornography in the workplace.
- Allowing sexual stereotyping in evaluating the performances of men and women.
- Leaving the solution of the problem to the management team that discriminated.
- Tolerating small transgressions.

Many women who are harassed, initially respond by trying to ignore the problem. But seventy-five percent of the time, harassment grows worse when it is ignored. Most victims don't want to file lawsuits. They simply want the harassment stopped. The following tactics can help stop the harassment.

1. Tell the harasser to stop. Make it clear you don't welcome this behavior. You can say this in person or in a letter (refer to the Appendix for a sample letter.) Keep copies of any written correspondence.

2. Keep notes describing each incident, including date, time, place, what the harasser said or did, how you responded, who else might have heard or seen it and what you did at the time. Keep these notes at home. Also, keep any gifts or notes you've received from the harasser.

3. Talk to others at work, even though it may be embarrassing. Be judicious about talking to your co-workers so you don't encourage gossip or possible harmful actions by others. You may find witnesses, allies or other victims of the harasser who will support you. It may be helpful as well to talk about the experience with friends and family.
4. Follow grievance procedures outlined in your company's employee handbook, if one exists. Talk to your supervisor, the harasser's supervisor, your union steward and any co-worker you think might be helpful. Remember, stopping sexual harassment is the responsibility of the employer as well as the harasser.
5. Keep copies of your employment record at home. Harassers sometimes try to defend themselves by attacking their victim's job performance.
6. Explore legal options and support groups. If other remedies fail, you may want to file a complaint.

Many complaints can be resolved informally using company grievance procedures. To take formal legal action under federal law, you must first file a charge with an administrative entity, such as the local Equal Employment Opportunity Commission (EEOC) or other appropriate state or local agency. Do this as soon as possible—no later than one hundred eighty days after the harassment occurs. You can locate the office nearest to you by looking in the telephone book or by calling (800) 669-4000.

You will need to talk to an intake worker who will discuss your charges and inform you of your rights and the filing procedure. Next, you need to fill out a complaint form, spelling out your charge. An investigator will notify your employer within ten days. (It's illegal for a company to retaliate against an employee who makes a discrimination complaint.)

Charges take an average of 283 days to be resolved. If the EEOC decides that you were harassed, your employer is required to remedy the situation, or to place you in the position you would have had if the discrimination had never occurred. You may also be entitled to monetary damages. If you think the damages are inadequate, or the EEOC decides not to pursue your case, you might want to consider hiring a lawyer to pursue a civil suit.

Chapter Ten

Recovering From Rape

Ellen came to counseling after she saw me on a TV appearance about my book, *Panic No More, Your Guide to Overcome Panic Attacks*. She said to herself, "She's the one who can help me." During her first counseling session, Ellen related she had been raped by a stranger several years ago. Since that time, she had suffered panic attacks and constant anxiety. She had changed her employment several times as a result of her anxiety.

Ellen feared seeing her attacker again. This fear followed her everywhere. She couldn't sleep well and had nightmares about the rape. Her only activity was going to church, where she still felt anxious.

Prior to the rape, Ellen was engaged to be married. She recounted that the rape occurred one night as she was coming home from a date. The electricity was off in her apartment. Her fiance thought something was suspicious and wanted her to spend the night somewhere else until the problem was corrected. Ellen refused and said she'd have it fixed in the morning.

After he left, Ellen started to undress and get ready for bed. She heard a voice say, "I've been watching you for a long time." Partly in shock, she started to scream. The man came out of the shadows and grabbed her. Ellen resisted, broke free and ran out of the apartment to her neighbor's door and started pounding on it screaming, "Let me in." Her friend never answered the door.

The man caught up with her and dragged her back into her apartment. This time he got a knife from the kitchen and put it to her throat. "Don't scream anymore, or I'll kill you," he threatened. Ellen could smell the alcohol on his breath. She feared for her life and decided to be docile and do what he told her.

The rapist ordered Ellen to get in bed where he raped her twice. Then he told her he was going to rape her once more in the morning, then kill her. Ellen lay quietly in bed thinking she was going to die. In the middle of the night, she heard a quiet voice inside her head tell her to ask him to go to the bathroom. He was foggy from the alcohol and sex. She asked. He nodded yes, she could go to the bathroom.

Ellen quickly stepped into the bathroom and grabbed a bath robe. Before he could catch her, she darted to the door and ran to a filling station for help. The police came and took her to the hospital for an exam. Ellen thought the police and emergency room personnel were very compassionate and helpful to her. They called her family and fiance. Unfortunately, the police never found the rapist.

Her fear had never left. In subsequent sessions, Ellen was taught how to mentally create a *safe place* inside herself. During hypnosis, she went back to the rape scene and relived it. She visualized her attacker behind bars where he couldn't hurt her. She also did the Eye Movement Therapy described in Chapter Fifteen.

Ellen made dramatic progress because she empowered herself by doing homework consisting of relaxation exercises, visualizations of a *safe place*, and creating self-calming statements and affirmations to repeat to herself during stressful times. She revisited the apartment where the rape occurred.

It took her nine sessions to overcome her Rape Trauma Syndrome and to relax her body enough to sleep soundly. Her anxiety diminished and gradually stopped completely. As she regained her perspective and sense of time, what turned out to be a rape a couple of years ago, was actually twenty years—of incredible anxiety and fear that her attacker would return and kill her.

One of the things Ellen identified as contributing to the trauma of the rape was that she had always felt "safe" in the world prior to the rape. Her early family life had been loving and supportive.

The rape, which totally overwhelmed her, changed her life view to that of the world being threatening and dangerous. Her fiance had been supportive right after the rape, but broke off the engagement a month later. Her friend, whose apartment she had gone to for help, later said she had heard her screaming, but refused to answer the door. Ellen learned this "friend" was jealous of her and wanted her fiance. Ellen felt betrayed and all alone. She could never feel safe after that and stopped dating.

Toward the end of her therapy, Ellen began going out and socializing more. She started drawing and painting, a hobby she had always liked, but never felt she had time for before.

HISTORY OF RAPE

Rape is an ancient crime. The word rape, comes from the Latin *raputs*, meaning "carrying off, abduction, or plunder." A woman was once owned as property by her father and sold by him to her husband, who then owned her. A rape perpetrated upon her was regarded as a crime against the male estate. Whomever owned her, her husband or her father, could sue and collect fifty pieces of silver because his "property" had been damaged.The fifty pieces of silver was the "fair market" price for the theft of virginity.

A rape could also result in marriage. In bride capture, a man could seize and rape a woman, and therefore acquire her as his property. Bride capture existed as a form of marriage in England as late as the fifteenth century.

In ancient Babylon, and in the Hebrew culture, a raped married woman was considered an adulteress and could be killed. Even in modern times, some husbands in Bangladesh turned from their raped wives in revulsion, considering their property abused and therefore at fault.

In wars throughout history, the rape of women has been part of the spoils of war. What better way to demoralize, humiliate and totally destroy all remaining illusions of power and property, than the rape of the conquereds' women?

Only recently, has a woman owned her body in marriage. Every state will now prosecute a husband for rape, with or without a marital rape law. Previously, having sex was a husband's right, whether his wife wanted it or not. But even if a woman is raped by her date or her husband, the rapist will probably "get off" as these type of rapes are very hard to prove.

Sixty to seventy percent of rapes occur because the man won't take "No" for an answer. He has planned to rape in advance, regardless of protest, and he just won't stop. Police hesitate to press charges and often dismiss these cases as "unfounded." They may believe a rape occurred but don't think they can get a conviction. As long as society blames the victim and fails to punish rapists and protect its victims, it condones rape and "enables" women to be victimized.

The violence against women—rape, domestic violence, childhood sexual abuse—are the direct result of male aggression. Men who consider women as "property," "whores," "virgins," "sluts," "bitches," and married women as "legal prostitutes" have little respect for women and view them as second class citizens. They feel entitled to vent their rage and anger, and blame women—and they use sex as a weapon. These men rape to gain power and control over women and put them down.

Women do not share the same freedom and independence as men. They cannot go where they want, whenever they want. Their freedom is suppressed by the threat of rape.

Rape is a hate crime. It is one of the most violent crimes in America—and it is also one of the most underreported crimes. Women living in large United States cities are more likely to be at risk for rape than anywhere else in the world.

The Justice Department estimates that fourteen percent of rapes are reported. Nationwide, there is a rape every five minutes. Some experts estimate two percent of them are ever reported, and only one percent of rape litigation results in a conviction. The National Victim Center and Crime Victims Research and Treatment Center, in *Rape in America: A Report to the Nation* (1992) gives the following statistics:

- 12.1 million American women alive today have been raped.
- 1/3 of the rapes occurred when the victims were less than 11 years old.
- An additional 1/3 were raped between the ages of 12 and 17.
- 8 in 10 rape victims knew the person who raped them.
- 1 in 10 rapes involved a boyfriend or ex-boyfriend.
- 1 in 4 were raped by a relative who was not a spouse.
- 1/2 of rape victims were fearful of injury or death during the rape.
- 1 in 6 victims reported to the police being raped.
- Of victims who reported the rape, the majority did so within 24 hours of the rape.
- 7 in 10 victims were afraid of their families finding out they had been sexually assaulted and people thinking it was their fault.
- 3 times as many rape victims as non-victims are depressed.
- Rape victims are 4 times more likely than non-victims to contemplate suicide and 13 times more likely to attempt suicide.

Compare these national figures with Tulsa, Oklahoma, a city of 384,000, selected as the most average city in America in 1994. The Tulsa Institute of Behavioral Sciences sponsored, *Rape: Tulsa Women Speak Out* in 1993 and discovered:
- 3 in 10 Tulsa women have been raped.
- 7 in 10 rape victims were younger than 20 years old when they were raped.
- 3 in 10 Tulsa women were molested as children.
- Overall, 50% of women living in Tulsa have been sexually abused at some point in their lives.
- 8 in 10 rape victims know the person who raped them.

- 2 in 10 rapes involved date rape type situations.
- 3 in 4 men used physical force to rape their victims.
- 1 in 2 rapes involved the use of drugs or alcohol.
- 4 in 5 victims did not report being raped to the police.
- Most who did not report said they were too embarrassed to report it.
- 1 in 5 victims reported the crime to the police.
- 9 in 10 victims who reported did so because they wanted the rapist to be punished.
- Most reporting victims felt the police believed them and treated them with respect.
- 3 in 4 are glad they reported the rape.
- Educated, affluent and employed women were less likely to report being raped.
- Victims were 2 1/2 times more likely to report rapes by strangers.
- The more violent the rapist, the more likely the victim was to report the rape.

Why don't women report rape more often? Those who are raped by strangers are more apt to report the rape, especially if it was a brutal rape. But women raped on dates where alcohol or drugs were used, often delay seeking help and are more reluctant to report the crime.

They may not report it because they know the rapist. They may feel embarrassment, shame and guilt and question if they brought it on themselves. Some wonder if rape actually occurred. They may fear others won't believe them and be angry at them. Or they may minimize, "it wasn't that serious."

The rape trials of William Kennedy Smith, a young doctor, and Mike Tyson, heavyweight boxing champion, both examples of date rape, showed the nation in 1991 and 1992 what is involved in date rape legal procedures, and how traumatic and confusing it is to the victim. Mike Tyson was parolled from prison in 1995.

Women often report that their experience with the legal system is like being raped all over again. They must repeat their story several times to different officials, and also be medically examined to secure evidence for later litigation. They may even be required to take a lie detector test.

It's important for a woman reporting a rape to know that the case belongs to the state—not the victim. The victim is a witness in the case against the offender. It takes approximately one to three years from the arrest of the perpetrator to conviction. That's a long time to put your life on hold, but it's necessary to bring the rapist to justice. Each time a rapist is convicted, all women win in their effort to gain total freedom and peace of mind.

Many victims emerge from a rape trial with anger and resentment toward a legal system that seems to "protect the criminal and condemn the victim." Given the nature of rape cases, there is a distinct possibility that the offender will go free. If this happens, the victim has the right to sue the rapist for damages. Such action would be a civil case rather than a criminal one.

In a civil action, the burden of proof (preponderance of evidence) is somewhat less stringent than is required in a criminal trial (beyond a reasonable doubt), and it is only necessary to establish that the victim suffered harm as a result of the defendant's action. A unanimous jury verdict is not required for the victim to win, and third parties can also be sued (e.g. fraternities, businesses) who failed to provide a safe environment that would prevent rape. Civil action will not put the rapist in jail, but it can result in a judgement. The victim is responsible for retaining a lawyer and absorbing legal fees.

Some of the reasons so little is done about prosecuting rapists are the myths and old beliefs about rape that permeate our culture.

MYTH vs REALITY*

Myth	Reality
It could never happen to me.	All kinds of people have been raped. Any age, race, class, religion, occupation, education, or physical description of people are at risk.
Most rapes occur as a "spur of the moment" act in a dark alley by a stranger.	Rape often occurs in one's home. Over 60-70 percent of the time, the offender is a relative, friend, neighbor, date, or other acquaintance of the victim. Even when the rapist is a stranger, the rape is usually planned in advance.
Rape is a sexual crime.	Rape is a crime of violence, of the need to overpower and control, dominate and humiliate another person. Satisfying a "sex drive" is not behind the act. In fact, most rapists have consenting sexual partners.
A rapist is easy to identify. He stands out in a crowd.	Most rapists appear to be normal people. Most are married and young, although they can be any age. They can also be of any race, color, and socioeconomic class.

*Adapted from the Oklahoma Coalition Against Domestic Violence and Sexual Assault

Rape only happens to young women	Rape victims range in age from 2 months to 106 years. Rape is an act of force. Anyone can be a victim.
People who are raped "ask for it" by their dress or actions.	Research shows that rapists look for women who are perceived as vulnerable, not people who dress in a particular way. No person asks to be hurt or degraded, just as no one asks to be robbed because they are carrying money in their pocket. Rape is the responsibility of the rapist, not the victim.
A person can't be raped if they don't want it.	Rape is a frightening, often life-threatening situation. Fear of death, threat of harm, or physical brutality can immobilize anyone, and make them unable to fight back.
Sexual assault is an individual act of deviance.	Rape is a societal problem with roots in our rape culture: it underscores the vast differences in power between women and men.

The way to end rape is for men to treat women with respect and equality. Rape can affect a woman for the rest of her life. Some women react by going out and having sex just to see if they're still "normal." Others may not want to be touched in a sexual way at all, but may only want to be held. It takes an average of four years to overcome the trauma of rape. Many relationships do not survive the stress.

RAPE TRAUMA SYNDROME

The Rape Trauma Syndrome was coined in 1974 by Ann Burgess and Lynda Holmstrom in a historic study of rape victims at Boston City Hospital. The Rape Trauma Syndrome is a form of Posttraumatic Stress Disorder (PTSD), and is characterized by three phases many (but not all) victims encounter.

The first phase can last from a few hours to a month. In this phase, victims are in shock, and exhibit extreme emotional upset and feelings of anger, guilt, fear, humiliation, revenge, anxiety, guilt, embarrassment, self-blame and often disbelief. They may feel powerless and vulnerable and wander about in a daze. Other victims, having been taught that anger is unacceptable, may appear calm, smiling or restless, while their insides are shaking apart.

Fears and nightmares associated with the rape make sleep elusive. The victims may appear confused, uncertain, inconsistent and may have memory lapses. It is difficult for them to make simple decisions. Hypervigilance is constant. They are raw from fear.

Physical symptoms include bleeding, soreness, trembling, bruising, pain, rapid breathing, headaches, fatigue, tension, nausea, tight muscles, numbness, loss of appetite and sleep disturbances such as nightmares and flashbacks. Most victims isolate and withdraw from their larger circle of friends. They take some "turtle time" and pull into a shell while healing and regrouping defenses. After a while, they think enough is enough, and decide it's time to get on with life. This entrance back into the world marks the beginning of the second phase.

The victim may even announce that she is "over" the rape. She then tries to understand the rape as a "bad experience." She reasons that she has had other bad experiences and recovered. She returns to work and resumes her life as lover, parent and partner. She tries to connect again with people and things that were important to her before the rape. But she is forever changed. The rape has affected her more deeply than she thought. If she had been sexually abused in childhood, the rape will probably cause these memories to surface. Then she will have two traumas to deal with instead of one. All her assumptions about the world as a just and safe place are shattered by rape.

If she thinks bad things only happen to bad people, then she may think the rape was punishment for something she did wrong. She may feel guilty for having been violated. It's not only common for the victim to blame the victim, but other people as well, through their own ignorance and beliefs about rape myths.

It's inevitable that things go wrong. Her confidence lags. She's unsure. She questions everything. Her body is stressed and depleted from the hyperviligance. Slowly her energy level drops and she feels tired and wants to sleep. Lethargy sets in as the dark cloud of depression grows. She may not relate the changes in her health and behavior to the rape.

The third phase is marked by depression, anxiety, fear, insomnia, nightmares, and tension headaches, the same as before. Some victims become so depressed that they attempt suicide. Relationships undergo the greatest stress at this time because she appears to be "getting worse instead of better."

Seventy-five to eighty-five percent of married women who are raped are divorced two years later. Often times, their husbands may blame them for the rape, or feel they are "tainted" and no longer attracted to them. They don't understand the grave seriousness of what has happened.

If She Is Raped, A Guidebook for Husbands, Fathers and Male Friends, by Alan McEvoy and Jeff B. Brookings, published by Learning Publications, Inc. Dept Q, is an excellent reference. The book helps educate and explain to the significant other what the victim is going through.

Victims are never responsible for the behavior of the rapist. The fact that the victim survived the rape means that she did the right thing. The average time it takes a rape victim to recover is approximately four years. During this time many changes are occurring. A new world view develops. New friendships are made, jobs change, and a tendency emerges to be more cautious and less trusting of people she has not known for a long time. Long delayed hobbies are revived. Each day is lived as a new challenge.

EFFECTS OF SEXUAL VIOLENCE

Rape affects all of us, as a society. When one woman is raped, we all feel unsafe. Read over the following effects of sexual violence and see how many ways sexual violence has affected you.

Victims
Isolation from others, depression
Increased alcohol and other drug abuse
Lost work time, decreased productivity, lost wages
Emotional problems, intense anger, low self-esteem
Illness, including sexually transmitted diseases and HIV; injury
Unwanted pregnancy
Suicidal thoughts or attempts
Relationship problems
Divorce
Guilt and shame

Sexuality issues
Generalized fear, especially of men
Feelings of helplessness and loss of control
Anxiety disorders, phobias and panic attacks
Sleep disturbances, nightmares, flashbacks
Intrusive thoughts
Decrease or increase in appetite, weight gain or loss, eating disorders

Loved ones
Guilt for not protecting the victim
Intense anger
Feelings of helplessness
Confusion about how to help the victim
Sexuality issues
Increased fear, overprotectiveness of the victim
Relationship problems
Divorce
(Loved ones may experience a range of emotions and difficulties
similar to those of the primary victim)

Employers
Lowered employee productivity
Absenteeism
Costs of rehiring and retraining new employee if victim quits
Reluctance of employees to take on certain tasks due to fear of crime
Guilt over firing employee for her reduced productivity

Society
Legal and criminal justice costs
Cost of prison
Climate of fear (often of all men by women)
Medical and counseling expenditures

Societal violence
Generalized feelings of helplessness and powerlessness
Generalized fear of "moral decay"
Anger and depression

PROFILE OF MEN WHO RAPE

Contrary to popular opinion, most rapists don't just jump out of the bushes and rape. Sixty to seventy percent of all rapes are by someone the victim knows.

The rapists are often young men, (although they can be any age), who plan in advance how they will get the unsuspecting victim alone. For example, he may take you out on a date and buy you a meal. He may try and get you to drink some alcohol to put you in a compromised condition. When he takes you home, he feels justified in raping you because he spent some money on you. Actually, any excuse will do. He may say you flirted with him and were "asking for it." Rapists feel little remorse for the rape, and will rape again and again.

The rapist may stalk his victim for some time before attacking her. Again contrary to popular opinion, sex is not the primary motive. The rapist is looking for a female to overpower, dominate and humiliate, in order to make himself feel masculine and adequate. He has no respect for women and the rape is his way of achieving "male dominance."

Gangs that "set up" a female to gang rape as a way of "male bonding" are also depreciating the female. They view her as an inferior being that they can kick around, humiliate and rape to prove to each other their masculinity and superiority. When males gang rape, they engage in a type of veiled homosexual contact with each other by "sharing" the same female. This type of attack is likely to be brutal and the victim sustains many injuries.

147

America is a rape culture, and rape is an All American Sport with aggressive males. Although there are statutes in every state against rape, the chances of a rapist being convicted are slim. Only one percent of rapists are convicted.

With little to deter rapists, they go on to become serial rapists. Raping makes them feel good, as if they are in control, which reinforces their distorted sense of masculinity. They are thus rewarded for raping and have little chance of punishment. After they have raped six or seven women, as their anger intensifies and the violence escalates, most rapists start killing their victims.

SELF-DEFENSE

Women can learn how to fight back and stop taking the old victimizing advice—that fighting back can endanger a woman's life. It's in danger anyway. Take self-defense courses such as karate or IMPACT Self-Defense or Model Mugging to learn how to protect yourself.

In 1991, fifty graduates of IMPACT and Model Mugging programs were attacked. Thirty-seven of them knocked out their attackers within five seconds. Eleven escaped without knocking out the assailant and two chose not to fight because their assailants had weapons (Aburdene and Naisbitt, 1992). Fighting back can and does make a difference—if you know how.

Chapter Eleven

Anger,
Denial
and
Depression

Victim of a victim
I'm standing up to the storm of your thrashing anger
Your assaults on me melt against my loving hand

Victim of a victim
I stand accused of indifference
As I stand steady in the center of your deluge,

peppered by your insults,
whipped by your rage

Victim of a victim
I watch you flee everything proud and noble
all that's strong and kind

I watch you flee
Like water down a rusty basin drain
To that human slag
Who squat just below
Your riddled sense of self-esteem

Victim of a victim
I let you try to bruise me
and whittle at my pride
because I love the soul that's trapped inside
this awful spiral of pain

Victim of a Victim was written by a young man who came to therapy to work on his relationship with a young woman, the victim of sexual violence. His own pain and suffering are described in the poem. And like so many others who have relationships with wounded women, the justified rage and anger the victim feels is often turned against their loved ones.

One reason anger is dumped on loved ones is that the victim feels safer and more secure in their presence, and therefore it is easier to express emotions. The abuser may not be available (as in a rape) or the victim may not feel safe (an employer or battering husband). The victim has no appropriate person to turn to vent her rage. Significant others who feel the sting of her anger need to know it is misdirected anger and should not take it personally.

Anger is a normal human emotion, and anger about being abused is normal. All victimized people are angry about the wrong done to them, whether they acknowledge it or not. Expressing that anger in healthy ways is part of empowerment, healing, and taking back power from the offenders and perpetrators. Anger is an extremely volatile source of energy. When that energy is externalized in positive ways, it usually manifests in a creative process.

Likewise, unexpressed, repressed anger is very destructive to your overall health and well being. It will present itself in various ways until you address it—or the anger may eventually destroy you if you continue in denial. When you internalize the anger, it often turns into some sort of degenerative process. These can include numerous somatic and stress related illnesses, and maladaptive behaviors, such as suicidal behavior, alcoholism, overeating and even "bruxation" (where you grind your teeth and keep the mouth clamped tightly shut—so you can't talk about what's going on inside).

Anger is one of the most difficult emotions for women to feel and express because of their traditional female socialization to be passive, people pleasers and look to males as smarter and more powerful. Many women, born and reared in a patriarchal society, take on the prevailing myths of the culture. Some never stop to question them. Are males really smarter, superior, or know more than females? Some women try hard to protect the male fragile ego. Why bother?

A person who doesn't have boundaries can't express anger. Without boundaries, you either go into a rage, or compensate for anger by being nice, and trying to please others, so you won't be confronted. This is the way millions of women have been culturally conditioned to repress anger and please others.

When anger is never expressed directly, nothing ever gets

resolved. The same argument may go on for twenty years in a family. A wife spills hot coffee in her husband's lap and says it's an accident. Frigidity and impotence are about anger, not sex.

Women are trained to nurture, protect and be there for others—but not for themselves. This scripting makes women victims. Some women even blame themselves when something goes wrong. "It must have been my fault I was hit . . . raped . . . harassed . . . . By accepting responsibility for others, these women participate in their own victimization.

Each time you deny your feelings, or blame yourself, or make excuses for the inappropriate behaviors of others, you turn anger in on yourself. When you refuse to talk about it, press charges, or blow the whistle, you further your own victimization and that of all women.

Anger expressed by women is usually not welcomed or accepted. In fact, anger is often discouraged, if not an out-and out-punishable, offense. One client told a story whereby her mother washed out her mouth with soap every time she expressed anger. By the time she came for therapy in her late twenties, she was emotionally numb and had no idea how she felt. Her only clue that she was angry was a skin rash, and the biting edge of her teeth were worn down past the enamel.

Another client equated feeling and expressing anger as offending God and being unchristian. Her family and their version of religion effectively controlled and manipulated her. They used her as the family peacemaker (a thankless job), and the family doormat. Her symptoms included numerous fears such as never being good enough, and repressed anger, which manifested in stomach irritation and colon problems. She was conditioned to be a martyr, and like most martyrs, if you scratch the surface, you find a seething, raging, volcano of anger underneath.

Inappropriate role models for the healthy expression of anger leave many women wondering if they even have a right to feel anger. When women do express their anger, they are often labeled "bitch," "selfish," "mean," "unthoughtful" or some other equally degrading term.

If anger was viewed as unacceptable while growing up, you may feel guilty for even getting angry. You may get so good at repressing anger you are unaware of any signs of it, except "feeling bad." Stuffing anger doesn't make it go away.

Stuffing anger most often occurs within a family culture where feelings are not allowed or where the right to express anger is prohibited by a very angry/controlling parent. "Stuffers" may not be aware that they have the *right* to be angry. Stuffing is a learned behavior, and it can be unlearned.

BEVERLY

Beverly grew up in a family that taught the children they could only express "acceptable emotions." Her parents could express their anger, but not the children. When she was a small child, her father repeatedly told her how disappointed he was that she was born female. "I wanted a son to carry on my name and leave my business to. When you were born a girl, I got drunk for a week." When Beverly complained about his down putting, her mother said, "Be quiet. Your father is a decent man and he makes a good living for us."

When Beverly was eleven, her father was looking at some family pictures that had recently been taken of his two daughters. He did not recognize Beverly and asked her older sister, "Carol, who is your good looking friend?" Carol replied, "Beverly." Her father looked astonished at Beverly, as if he had never seen her before. Beverly had always hoped her father would notice her and give her the love and affection she craved from him.

What he noticed was that she was sexually maturing. Shortly after this scene at the family dinner table with the pictures, Beverly's father came home from work unexpectedly. It was afternoon, and her sister, Carol, and her mother were at a violin lesson. He told Beverly to come up to his bedroom. He then unzipped his pants, threw her down on the bed, put his penis into her mouth and proceeded to ejaculate in her mouth. Her father threatened her with death if she ever told anyone.

Beverly wondered what she had done that could have been so bad to deserve that kind of punishment. Afterwards, he frequently referred to her as a "bitch" and a "whore." Since he referred to her in this way, Beverly thought it must be the truth. To this list of derogatory labels, Beverly added "bad," "tainted" and "worthless."

Beverly repressed the incident, and the many that followed. She could never think of her father as an abuser, or doing anything wrong. In her mind, and as she had been taught, her father was "perfect" and "always right." It was the children who were "bad."

Beverly tried harder to be good to make up for her feelings of worthlessness. She worked hard at her school work and made A's. She tried to please people so they would like her, tried to help others, to be Christian, and in a million other ways pay off her endless debt of bad karma.

When she married, her husband verbally abused her. He pushed her around and demeaned her. When their son was born, he also abused him. Beverly didn't take up for herself, but she did for her son, and she divorced his father.

Years later, Beverly remarried (Chapter Three). She thought Bob would be a good father for her son. This husband also abused Beverly by running around with other women, and pushing and shoving her into walls. Several times he pulled out his pistol and threatened to kill her. That marriage also ended in divorce.

At one job, Beverly's boss sexually harassed her. She finally quit to get away from the harassment. Things didn't get much better. Beverly was date raped one evening. She got the idea something must be wrong with her for so many bad things to happen.

By this time in her life, she had developed serious headaches. Every year in the fall, she would be "taken sick" and go to bed for a week. During this time she would convulse, her body would seizure and her head would throb with pain. Then, just as suddenly as it started, it would end, until the next year about the same time. The attacks coincided with her first sexual abuse by her father, even though she had no memory of it until later in her therapy.

When her father died, Beverly experienced the happiest day of her life. She felt as thought a giant weight had been lifted from her soul and described it as "all the anger I never knew I had leaving my body."

At the time of her father's death, Beverly had not recalled her childhood memories. A short time later, the anger, depressed mood, and aches and pains, returned to, once more, weigh her down. Her mother's death several years later, triggered nightmares and flashbacks about the sexual abuse.

Beverly came to therapy while she was married to Bob. It took several years of therapy for her to come to terms with all that she had been through as a child. She had to encounter her own anger and define it as justifiable, before she could stop being a victim.

As long as her anger remained repressed, it was a blind spot where further boundary violations and victimizations occurred without notice. After Beverly experienced her anger at her father, then she recognized victimizing treatment from abusive men. She had to learn the ingredients of a healthy relationship with a man.

WHEN ANGER IS INTERNALIZED

For women, when anger has been squelched in childhood, it is usually turned inward. For most men, anger is projected onto others and the environment. Women need to learn how to express anger in positive ways. Abusive men need to learn how to manage and control their anger. The expression of anger and its management is a highly individualized matter. There is not a simple formula about how to do it. Anger, and what causes it, is not the same for everyone.

Repressed, unexpressed anger can turn into self-destructive, self-defeating behaviors, and symptoms such as depression, headaches, arthritis, and numerous stress related illnesses such as cancer, hypertension, and ulcers.

Women usually end up going to doctors and hospitals for their various ailments. If the depression becomes severe enough, suicidal thoughts are not uncommon. The unexpressed anger and just feeling bad creates, in addition to the pain of victimization, the feelings of being trapped and helpless.

When you are overcontrolled and punished in childhood for acting independently and/or expressing anger, in adulthood you may do your own punishing. You can do this by inducing headaches or other ailments. Somatization (turning unacceptable thoughts and emotions into symptoms) may become a conditioned response.

When this occurs, anger is suppressed at the subconscious level, while consciously, your head pounds as if there is a war going on inside. You have internalized your critical parent, and that part of you is still meting out the punishment. Practice acceptance of your feelings. If you remain psychologically unaware, you may spend time and money going to different doctors trying to find a physical cause for the pain.

SYMPTOMS OF DEPRESSION

Due to societal conditioning, depression is a natural outcome for women who have been victimized. In fact, if you go to the emergency room or see a doctor about being battered, raped or stressed out at work due to sexual harassment, you are most likely to be handed a prescription for a tranquilizer to help you get over it. How does that help you deal with the anger? It doesn't. Most often, the anger turns to depression.

Read over and check off the following list of symptoms of depression. If you have checked more than four of the symptoms, you are probably depressed.

1.____ Are you experiencing feelings of sadness?
2.____ Have you lost interest in the future?
3.____ Do you feel like a failure?
4.____ Do you feel like you're being punished?
5.____ Do you hate yourself?
6.____ Do you feel unattractive?
7.____ Has your sex drive decreased?
8.____ Has your appetite changed (increase or decrease)?
9.____ Have you had a recent weight loss or weight gain?
10.____ Have you lost interest in people or activities?
11.____ Are you experiencing feelings of helplessness or despair, often accompanied by tearfulness?
12.____ Are you worried about your health?
13.____ Do you have sleep disturbances (sleeping more or less)?
14.____ Do you have loss of energy or general fatigue?
15.____ Do you have feelings of guilt or worthlessness?
16.____ Are you indecisive?
17.____ Do you have trouble concentrating?
18.____ Do you have recurrent thoughts of death or suicide?

DENIAL

Women are masters at denying anger. They clench their teeth, have rashes, upset stomachs, dull, gnawing headaches, gastritis attacks, and feel very, very tired. They may blame it on something they ate. Depression covers the deep anger and pain over the loss of the self that results from denial. Depression is a socially acceptable way for women to deal with their anger.

Aggressive, angry, acting out men may not get sick, but they usually wind up in jail due to taking their anger out on others and society. Research studies of male prisoners shows most were abused in childhood, and those awaiting execution for murder had been sexually abused.

Anger is a healthy function of the body, mind, and soul. It's a message that something is terribly wrong with what is going on. Anger is an energy and a vehicle to regain your power, self-respect, self-esteem and self-control, and say, "It is unacceptable to yell at me, push me around, or tell nasty jokes at my expense. This will never happen to me again. If you choose to continue in the behavior, I will leave"—and mean it and do it. If you make empty threats nothing will happen. You will lose faith in yourself and your self-esteem will sink even lower.

When you deny anger, it is like saying, "I am unworthy of decent treatment." Your self-esteem plummets, and you take one more step further into the *victim role*.

After an assault, it's possible for a previously passive type person to identify with the aggressor—and flip over into an aggressive style of expressing herself. That's probably the only other option that has been role modeled for her.

People who have been victimized frequently may overreact to a situation. As one woman put it, "I just wait for someone to cross me so I can let them have it."

FEAR OF ANGER

Are you afraid you might lose control if you express anger? Hit someone? Break something? Say something you will regret later?

People commonly confuse anger, which is an emotion, with an action, which is an abusive behavior. In the Battered Woman Syndrome, the abused woman reaches the breaking point. Full of fear and rage, she kills her battering husband in self-defense.

Phil Hyde, MS-CTRS at Laureate Psychiatric Hospital and Clinic says, "Often, it is hard to separate emotions from behaviors. As you become more trusting of your own intuition and body's messages, you can better understand your own anger and intervene in your own behalf. Just because you're angry doesn't mean you have to do anything about it physically. Learn to put it into words and release it that way."

What if you're afraid of hurting someone's feelings by talking about your angry feelings? If so, you may rationalize that you might offend or hurt someone else and refuse to talk to them. Remember, you are only responsible to communicate what you think and feel.

You are not responsible for what others feel, or do with your communication. How they take it is their choice, their right, and their responsibility. Trying to protect others from your feelings is falling into the codependency trap.

Another way of negating anger, is to retreat from honest communication. Here you may avoid direct confrontation by communicating through a third party, or simply deny that you are angry. You may have never learned to recognize the bodily manifestations of anger, (reddening of the face, mouth clamping shut, grinding teeth, fist pounding), or you may not even equate screaming and throwing things with feeling angry.

If you are unaware of your feelings, or do not know how to express anger, what will probably happen is that rage, instead of anger, will come out when you talk about your anger. It's like you turn on the water faucet, but the handle breaks off in your hand and the water gushes everywhere.

If you have difficulty modulating the expression of your feelings, practice identifying and expressing all your feelings. This will help you develop a self that can safely and effectively express anger. Learn to identify and control the expression of your feelings and how to turn them on, and off, with your will. Don't be a leaky faucet.

NEED FOR PROTECTION

Victims who have been traumatized, overwhelmed, and made to feel powerless and helpless, may adopt new beliefs based on that perspective when they rebuild their shattered world. They may also feel the need for protection, especially if they've never been adept at expressing anger or being assertive. They may develop Posttraumatic Stress Disorder where they are always on guard for further assaults, and constantly scan the environment to "fight or flee" from danger.

After chronic fatigue sets in (from always being on guard), victimized women may lash out at anyone whom they perceive as a threat, or they may simply cower in silence, hoping the (d)anger will pass.

There is a fine line between helping the victim regain control of her world and becoming overprotective. Too much help from loved ones shields the victim from having to confront her own anger. This can lead to crippling dependency and further entrench her in the *victim role*.

The more helplessness and powerlessness that is condoned

for the victim, the more you encourage her to become a professional victim. It will be much more beneficial to encourage her to take as much control of her life as she can.

Assertiveness

Those individuals who have grown up passive due to childhood training and/or victimization—can benefit from a course in assertiveness training to help them learn to verbally protect themselves. By learning the different styles of communication, and how to express anger positively without infringing on the rights of others, the victim can quickly step out of the *victim role* and regain her sense of self-worth and self-esteem.

Assertiveness is a communication style that respects yourself and respects the rights of others. It includes making "I" statements and expressing *directly* how you feel and what you think.

For example, "I would appreciate it if you would allow me to make my own decisions as to whom I'm going to tell about the rape." "I realize you said I shouldn't wear low cut dresses. However, that's your opinion as to what caused me to get raped, and that's all it is—your opinion. The facts are, rapists seek out women who are perceived as vulnerable." "It's my opinion that taking a self-defense course will help me." "I want us to get some counseling before our relationship is hurt."

When you assert yourself, avoid blaming, interpreting, diagnosing, labeling, preaching and putting the other person down. True assertiveness respects the rights and human dignity of others.

Role playing is an important exercise when learning assertiveness. Ask a friend to rehearse a scene with you before you do a "live" assertion. Be specific about what you want and need. Do not assume the other person already knows what you want. Also role play the person with whom you wish to be assertive, to determine the effectiveness of the assertion.

EXPRESSING ANGER CREATIVELY

The following exercises can help you get in touch with your anger and express it in positive ways.

- One of the most effective ways for victimized women to get in touch with their anger and rage, is to paint the face of the perpetrator on a pillow. Hit it, stomp on it, scream at it, and tear it apart.

- Another way to externalize anger is to talk to an empty chair, as though the abuser was sitting in it. Talk out all your feelings about the abuse. Say, "What I felt at the time was ____." "What I feel now is ___." "What I want you to do for me now is___." This is a good exercise to practice prior to confronting an abusive situation or abuser.

- Writing down your feelings about anger is also helpful. The act of writing helps to integrate your feelings and experiences. You usually can't discharge the energy until it has been fully integrated, so writing is very important. It also helps you separate out the different emotions you have so you can understand and deal with them better.

- Visualize the abuser behind bars, where he can't hurt you anymore. Tell yourself, "I am safe." Only after you feel completely safe will you be able to get in touch with all your anger—and your healing.

- Painting your angry emotions on canvas or wood is also a good exercise. You don't need fancy brushes or lessons. You can smear on the paint with your fingers. When you're finished, step back and look at what you've painted. One client painted her emotions this way and brought her art work to therapy. It was a beautiful piece of art that showed the anger trying to surface from underneath black blockages of fear and repression.

Art therapy works wonders. Long recognized as the conductor between mystical inner worlds and outer realities, art therapy can reach anger, memories and fears you may be unable to verbally express.

- Molding with clay is also helpful. At a treatment center for sexual abuse, several women each molded a penis with clay, then smashed it apart. It helped them get in touch with their anger and release it in an atmosphere of love and trust.

- Learn to set boundaries with yourself and others. Eventually, you may want to confront your abuser and tell him what is acceptable and unacceptable to you. When you do this, tell him that you are a worthwhile person, and that treating you with disrespect, has consequences. Then explain to him what they are. In that way you take back control of your life.

- Take a women's self-defense course (usually offered at vocational training centers, community centers or colleges). Imagine your trainer is the perpetrator/offender, and really get into the attack scene. Trainers can handle your aggressiveness, so don't be afraid to really "let go."

- Expressing righteous indignation and anger at being abused is a must. This step in the healing process cannot be bypassed. You are entitled to your anger. Express it!

SHOULD YOU FORGIVE

Contrary to popular opinion, you don't have to forgive the abuser. You do need to express your anger, rather than stuff it while keeping a nice sweet smile on your face. Eventually, you only need to accept what happened. The anger will probably fade of its own accord during the acceptance phase.

Trying to be loving toward, or forgiving the offender, discounts all that you have been though. It's like saying the abuse never happened. If the offender has made no changes, there is nothing to forgive.

It's you who *eventually* needs to forgive yourself for holding the rage, anger, pain, resentment and revenge fantasies. Prior to the abuse, you had expectations that you would not be traumatized. These expectations held your world in place. The disappointment that these expectations were not met, led to the anger, pain and resentment. After you have satisfied yourself in processing and coming to terms with these feelings, then is the time to forgive yourself. Deep prayer or meditation is the best environment to do this in.

The same is true with "understanding." Even if the offender himself was a victim of child abuse, you're entitled to your anger. Being understanding short circuits your own developmental healing process and makes you feel guilty for your own feelings of anger and outrage. Knowing the abuser was also a victim may be a great intellectual exercise, but emotionally it will not help you one bit.

If you do not learn to express the anger, you will be confronted by it daily, one way or the other. You simply cannot escape it. You may have headaches. You may not be able to sleep. You may be victimized over and over. Your meal at the restaurant may be burned. You may get shortchanged at the supermarket.

If you continually avoid being assertive and expressing your anger, it builds up and one day you either find yourself thinking of suicide or homicide. Your emotional trigger will grow so fragile that a small, insignificant incident may send you into a rage. Don't let the dog or cat or the weather pull your trigger and send you "over the edge." You don't have to wait until something like that happens for you to seek treatment. You cannot avoid the responsibility for your life, setting your boundaries, and protecting yourself.

Be suspicious of the motives of anyone who is willing to take on boundary setting and responsibility for you, because they will have their own agenda. If you do not live and direct your own life, someone else will. Beware! Delegating and/or relinquishing the responsibility for your life can result in *viciousness*, *injury*, *crisis*, *torture*, *intimidation*, and never ending *mourning*.

• • •

Anger is one of the most important emotions for you to feel and work through to the fullest extent. Express all the righteous indignation and rage you can find inside yourself. In time, your anger may fade, or it may not.

This is your process to work through. Do not allow other people to talk you out of it by telling you, "You've been angry long enough. It's time to get on with your life." As long as you feel anger, it is there to teach you something. Listen to it. Learn from it. Grow from it. Your eventual goal is acceptance, not forgiveness.

Acceptance of the injustice done to you is a way out of the anger. When you can accept what has happened to you, and can accept the offender just as he/she is without wanting revenge or trying to help the abuser get better and reform, you are ready to move beyond the anger.

Chapter Twelve

Overcoming
Self-Destructive
Behavior

Karin stood among the throng at the convention, looking over the latest selection of health food books. Suddenly "he" appeared. Dressed in white from head to foot, his blonde hair neatly sculpted: he slipped her his card. Karin, surprised by the handsome stranger, couldn't believe the intense attraction between them. "I must be dreaming," she thought.

Over the next two months they wrote to each other, talked on the telephone, and made plans to meet at another convention in Philadelphia. When Karin stepped off the plane, there he was, big as life. It wasn't a dream. That night they made love and held each other close. It was then Russel told her he was in the process of a divorce. Karin rationalized his wife was only a short lived, minor inconvenience.

After the "honeymoon" in Philadelphia, Russel called Karin every night, professing his love. They arranged their next meeting in Aspen. Karin was surprised when Russel drove her to a new 5,000 square foot house overlooking the city. He mentioned there was some problem in the financial settlement with his wife, but not to worry.

He had purchased this new home for Karin—as a wedding gift, and would put it in her name when it was completed and landscaped. He told her the house was not in the divorce settlement, and that they needed to keep their relationship, and the house, a secret until the divorce was final.

They planned to be married as soon as his divorce came through and live in the house in Aspen. Karin, inspired by the intrigue and the romance, was hooked.

Over the next few months she flew to Aspen to help direct the workmen with the finishing touches. She picked out the carpet, wallpaper, marble for the fireplaces, and designed interiors of the kitchen and master suite for her new house. She worked on the lawn, pulled weeds and planted flowers in the garden. She and Russel enjoyed moonlit dinners, skied the mountains, and relaxed at the nearby hot springs spa. Karin was in love.

They also had romantic interludes in Denver, San Antonio, Orlando and San Francisco. A year went by. When Karin asked Russel how the divorce was coming, he said, "It's on hold. A financial settlement would kill me right now. It's just a matter of time until I can handle it." The house was completed. It seemed like a "dream come true." Karin decided to go ahead and move into the Aspen home, even though Russel was still living in Denver and still not divorced.

Russel told her he was tied up with business the date she planned to move, but he would meet her at the house as soon as possible. Karin quit her job and moved to the mountains. One week passed. No sign of Russel. Another week passed. He was in Philadelphia without her. His telephone calls became infrequent. When she asked Russel to go ahead and put the house in her name, he hedged. Early one morning, a real estate salesman knocked on the door with a couple who were interested in buying the house. The salesman assured her the house was for sale.

Karin felt abandoned. She had stomach cramps, headaches, nausea and vomiting. Her heart palpitated and she sweat profusely. She regretted her decision to quit her job and leave her family and friends—for the love of a man she realized she barely knew.

She felt used, helpless and powerless and at Russel's mercy. By this time, she had decided he had neither mercy nor morals, probably had numerous extramarital affairs, probably had conned people into doing free work for him before (such as weeding, planting and decorating a house), and would probably never get divorced. She feared being thrown out on the street, penniless.

Karin began to have flashbacks about the incest from her childhood. Out of control, in fear and panic, Karin fled the house. She never saw Russel again, although the repercussions of her actions followed her for years. She had difficulty finding another job and had to start all over at the bottom in her career.

Repetition Compulsion

Self-destructive behaviors often symbolically recreate the original trauma, clinically known as "repetition compulsion." This is what happened in Karin's case. In therapy, she later pieced the meaning of her behavior and her childhood abuse. She had fallen in love with a man who lied and betrayed her, just like her father. She had protected him by keeping his secrets.

Karin had recreated down to the last intrigue and secret, the trauma from her childhood incest, by an affair with a unavailable and forbidden married man. All the while, she thought she could win him, even though there were signs all along the way. Karin chose to hear only what she wanted to hear and see only what she wanted to see. Her rage, fears of abandonment, guilt, shame and disgrace, were triggered in her disillusionment when she found that Russel's promises meant nothing. Karin felt like a victim.

Russel had what is known as a "hothouse marriage." He controlled all the power and finances in his marriage. According to what Russel had told Karin, his wife was inadequate, helpless and had had several mental hospitalizations. Russel felt entitled; he was "to be pleased," both as an employer and a husband. He did whatever he wanted. Everyone else in his world was to do his bidding. He figured he didn't have to obey the same kind of laws as everyone else.

Russel had no reason to get a divorce because he could do anything he wanted—and he apparently loved the thrill of getting away with something. Several times during her therapy, Karin remembered Russel cheating and lying to salespeople over small things. She finally came to realize the extent of Russel's problems and her own revictimizing choices.

WHAT'S MISSING?

When a part of you has been emotionally criticized out of existence, denied, repressed, buried, or shattered, it will find some way of making itself known, either through the language of symptoms, or through the symbolic language of self-destructive behavior by attracting the conditions and situations in life to draw attention to the void. Self-destructive behavior is often compensatory behavior. It tries to make up for what's missing.

What's missing can include inadequate parenting. Where the parent is inconsistent, overly controlling, or nurtures poorly, the growing child is emotionally deprived and unable to develop normally. The child learns to deny the "unacceptable" aspects of the self and/or tries to take care of the inadequate parent in order to be loved and accepted and, therefore, survive.

Trauma and/or repression causes emotional numbing, constriction, and fragmentation of the personality. Affected people usually aren't in touch with their feelings or aware that a part of them is missing. They guess at what's normal and manufacture what they think are the "appropriate" feelings. By creating a mask, a facade, or an image to hide behind, they never know who or what they are. They just play roles.

Lost from their grounding core of spiritual, emotional and psychological life, they feel empty. John Bradshaw refers to this emptiness as the "hole in the soul." To try and fill the void, sufferers often turn to addictions and compulsions.

ADDICTIONS AND COMPULSIONS

Role playing and repression create enormous stress. People thus engaged often turn to addictions and compulsions to gain control over their seemingly endless pain, grief, stress and perceived nonexistence. They rely on the addictions and compulsions to alter moods, to fill the emptiness, and drive away feelings of worthlessness, sadness and depression.

Nurturing, modeling, and genetics, determine the type of addiction or compulsion: alcoholism, drugs, running, gambling, overwork (workaholism), rigid perfectionism, anorexia and bulimia, over-spending, sex, or addictive love. Most people who become addicted have more than one addiction. As a rule, the more severely a person is abused in childhood, the more addictions and compulsions they will have. Compensatory, self-destructive behaviors are enormously self-defeating, and can, in some cases, cause death.

Compulsive spending

Some people become compulsive spenders, buying material objects to compensate for their feelings of worthlessness. They want to feel and look as if they are "worth something." One man bought a sail boat so others would think he was a "real man." Because he tried to buy the appearance of success, he was usually broke and overloaded with debt. Many people in our society confuse worthiness with achievements and material success.

You are born worthy. True worthiness comes from acceptance of the self in all aspects. Achievements, material success, living in the "right" neighborhood or being married to the "right" person has nothing to do with worthiness. In fact, to pursue materialism and status to feel worthy produces even more feelings of emptiness and depression—and possibly a heart attack.

Whenever I hear a client say, "My life is full. I have a great job and husband, and all kinds of things people would die for. Why do I feel so empty and my life so meaningless?" I know she is trying to fulfill herself by "things" and "images" instead of being who she actually is.

Workaholics

Workaholics overwork to avoid their real feelings and compensate for their fears of unworthiness. Susan worked long, hard hours and took work home on the weekends. She didn't have much of a life, but when her coworkers praised her on what a fine job she did, her self-esteem rose . . . temporarily. Susan needed a steady supply of compliments to feel good about herself.

Eventually, she was promoted to the directorship of her department, and thus rewarded for her compulsion. All seemed to go well for awhile, but she became addicted to drugs, trying to relax. When Susan's health began to fail, she came to therapy to learn why she was living the way she was.

Susan traced her abuse back to her mother, who tried to live through her. Susan's mother had rigidly monitored her daughter's weight when she was growing up, administered daily enemas to her as a teenager, and even tried to get her to enlarge her breasts. Susan was made to feel, "never good enough." As Susan freed herself from her mother's control and developed a life of her own, her mother became extremely depressed. The mother was then forced to deal with the emptiness in her own life.

Many workaholics are extremely talented individuals who function well on an intellectual level. They may reach positions of authority and power in their work life, but feel very insecure emotionally and are frequently unable to sustain an emotional relationship in their personal life. They avoid themselves and their life by overworking.

Sexual addiction

Sexual addiction is out-of-control sexual behavior that tries to stop the pain from childhood abuse. Boundaries around sex are blurred and fused with fear and pain. Due to the isolation and emotional abandonment in families where abuse takes place, sexual feelings may become equated with loneliness.

Male sex addicts that do not understand they were abused in childhood may become remorseless sexual offenders. At a Veterans Hospital in California, seventy-three percent of the alcoholics in treatment were also found to have compulsive sexual issues. The following statistics of sex addicts reflect those abused in childhood:

- 81% were sexually abused
- 97% were emotionally abused
- 72% were physically abused

Some sex addicts in the California study, tried to limit their sexual contact by "white knuckling." But most spent an inordinate amount of time in obtaining sex, being sexual, or recovering from sexual experiences.

Important social, occupational or recreational activities are reduced because of the sexual addict's behavior and obsessive sexual fantasies. The result may be self-hatred and self- contempt, especially when faced with the consequences of that behavior.

Consequences include:
A.I.D.S.
loss of spouse - 40%
financial consequences - 58%
loss of career, demotion, or productivity - 27%
risk of sexually transmitted diseases - 65%
risk of arrest - 58%
unwanted pregnancies - 42%
grief over abortions - 36%

As with other addictions, sexual activity is an attempt to regulate moods, cope with depression and reduce stress. A common saying is "sex is my sleeping pill." Sexual addiction keeps you busy and distracted from the source of pain. It's a smoke screen that creates emotional distance, while mistaking intimacy for ecstasy. Intimacy involves communication, sharing oneself emotionally, and working through mutual problems. Sexual addiction involves sexual activity without emotional feelings—it's mechanical. Feelings are not involved. The partner is merely used as a convenience, then discarded like a wet blanket. Ironically, during sex may be the only time the addict feels close to another person. Like other addictions, the sexual activity increases because the current level is no longer sufficient.

There are several treatment centers that have special programs for sexual addicts. They include, but are not limited to, *Cottonwood* (800 877-4520) and *Sierra Tucson* (800 842-4487), both in Tucson, Arizona. After the initial treatment of approximately a month, the sexual addict may continue therapy as an outpatient.

Addictive love

As a child, The Love Addict is made to feel emotionally abandoned. The emotional emptiness is compensated by creating rescue fantasizes of The Magic One who will nurture, love and meet all needs.

These fantasies trigger endorphins that numb the emotional pain and make the abandoned child feel good, even loved and cherished. The result is an emotionally needy "adult-child," starving for love and affection.

When someone triggers the rescue fantasies, that person is instantly transformed into The Magic One, with all the accompanying images of goodness, hero and other godlike qualities. The object of their love rules their life. Sex is usually great (who wouldn't have great sex with a god!). The endorphins are released. The Love Addict mistakes this high feeling for love.

Consider what you would feel like if you had been subjected to the following circumstance. Your parent(s) are physically there but give you the unspoken message, "Don't have any needs because we don't have any time for them. Be quiet, be still, and don't bother me."

In this case, the parent may be emotionally unavailable due to focusing attention on an addictive spouse, may be addicted themselves, or working hard to support the family without any energy left for nurturing.

Another way of being emotionally abandoned is the situation where the parent(s) may either be sick, needy, or narcissistic—and assign you the responsibility of meeting their emotional needs instead of the other way around.

People who were deprived of having their own needs met while trying to meet the needs of their parents become Rescuers or Saviors when they grow up. They rescue troubled people; alcoholics, drug addicts, those with mental and emotional problems and/or those "down on their luck." They support them. Or they might find a married man whose wife doesn't understand him.

Rescuers often become professional psychics, social workers, nurses or other allied mental health professionals. If they don't get enough work on the job, they may also marry an addict and try to "fix" him by changing the addict into The Magic One. In the back of the Rescuer's and Saviour's minds is the fantasy fulfillment of the troubled partners getting strong enough to take care of them—like their parent(s) never could.

Rescuers and Saviours need to be needed. Since they derived self-esteem from taking care of the parent(s), they learned the pattern of gaining self-esteem from taking care of troubled people. Also, if the partners need them enough, the partners can't abandon them like their parents did—or so the reasoning goes.

As the Love Addict becomes obsessive, possessive, and jealous of time and attention given to anyone else, The Magic One comes to feel like a victim and a prisoner. As the pressure mounts up to conform to the needs of the Love Addict, The Magic One realizes how emotionally needy the Love Addict actually is. It is then, that The Magic One usually takes flight.

This rejection subconsciously replays the Love Addict's original childhood abandonment. This time the Love Addict thinks it will be different, so The Magic One is pursued unrelentingly. The line may be crossed into self-destructive behavior.

The Love Addicts spend most of their time thinking about their lovers, money sending presents, energy driving by their residence, stalking the target, and threatening harm to themselves or the target of their obsession, if The Magic One won't return.

If the lover doesn't come back, all the anger and rage of the young abandoned child is triggered. The Magic One now becomes the enemy.

Rejected lovers have a tendency to become punitive, retaliatory and also dangerous. Some targets of Love Addicts solve the problem by changing jobs and moving far away where they cannot be found. Others may seek the assistance of the police by filing harassment and anti-stalking charges.

The outcome is usually different for the Rescuers whose troubled partners stay and drain them dry for years. Ironically, The Magic One, selected to fulfill all the Love Addict's dreams, usually has abandonment and intimacy fears. Avoidance techniques, such as distancing, are used to sabotage closeness and avoid getting enmeshed with the Love Addict. Either way, people who are susceptible to love addiction usually can't live with the object of their love, or without them.

The treatment for love addiction is the uncovering of the original issues of childhood abandonment, rejection and/or deprivation of love. This, of course, takes lots of courage and the assistance of a therapist. It is possible for love addiction to be overcome and mature into real love.

Rigid perfectionism

People with rigid perfectionism may seem emotionally cold. They often see other people as extensions of themselves, and attempt to control them and their environment through constant criticism. Nothing is ever good enough.

Perfectionistic people try to do everything perfectly. They project their impossible standards on everyone else that they can. They work very hard at being "good" and "perfect." In any given situation, they are going to be right and you will be wrong.

When you walk in their houses, you think you have stepped into "Better Homes and Gardens." Everything's arranged perfectly. You can eat off the kitchen floor it's so clean. Their appearance is perfect. Everything matches. Every hair is in place. If the hairdo is a casual look, every hair will be perfectly, but casually, placed. They walk perfectly. They talk perfectly. You can't find anything wrong with them. Everything's by the book—but it's their book.

Rigid perfectionism stifles creativity and spontaneity. These people never relax. Their lives are filled with endless duty, obligation and responsibility—and doing it "just right." Affected people worry constantly and wonder, will it ever be over?

At the heart of rigid perfectionism, as in other compulsions, is the compensation for feeling like a bad person and trying to make up for it by being good. The disorder may be carried to such an extreme that the person becomes a martyr trying to do everything just right.

If you meet someone fitting this description, run the other way unless you enjoy feeling inferior. If this description fits you, get into therapy—fast. If you're not giving yourself headaches, you're giving them to other people.

Childhood sexual abuse and/or emotional deprivation, is often found at the core of this disorder. Once you retrieve the childhood memories, you will know and accept that you're not a bad person at all. You can heal and relax. Allow yourself to be just who you are. You have nothing to prove. Enjoy being alive.

Compulsive eating, anorexia and bulimia

Eating disorders are both a social problem and a psychological problem. The diet industry is a $33 billion a year business. Ninety percent of those affected with eating disorders are women.

Our society is influenced by male domination that defines beauty for women. Millions of women, made vulnerable in childhood by detached or aloof parents, are left emotionally starving for attention. They try to find acceptance by being perfect—perfectly thin. They think once they are thin enough, someone will love them. Once they are even thinner, they will find happiness.

Sadly, their future rests in the lover they call food. Their primary relationship becomes the struggle with food. The focus on food provides a distraction from underlying issues of trust and intimacy. They become experts at delayed gratification. Someday love will happen for them—when they are thin.

Anorexics starve themselves. Bulimics binge when they can no longer stand their internal pressures, and then purge. Individuals with eating disorders go on the next diet, hoping it will work, and the next and the next.

Eating disorders are never about food. They are about feeding the hunger and emptiness inside. Those persons afflicted with eating disorders want to feel good about themselves; worthy, good enough, and acceptable. They abuse themselves with food. Eating is a metaphor for the way they live.

Many people with eating disorders also have a history of childhood sexual abuse. The anorexia stops the menses. The sufferer emotionally regresses to the level of a young and innocent child. Now she is in control of what goes into her body as she struggles to feel loved.

In bulimia, semi-starvation cycles with gorging and purging. The bulimic feels the emptiness of self, and tries to fill it with food. The food being stuffed down the throat serves, on the surface, to make her feel better. She stuffs her feelings down with food, while keeping her mouth busy so she can't talk about what's bothering her.

The American Anorexia and Bulimia Association states that anorexia and bulimia strike a million women every year, and girls are developing this disorder at younger and younger ages. Girls in the fifth grade are now developing anorexia and bulimia. Anorexia and bulimia have the poorest recovery rate of all the mental disorders. Many die from starvation or malnutrition, or from the side effects of the binging and purging.

The medical effects of anorexia include hypothermia, edema, hypotension, bradycardia (impaired heartbeat), lanugo (growth of body hair), infertility, and death. The medical effects of bulimia include dehydration, electrolyte imbalance, epileptic seizures, abnormal heart rhythm, and death. When the two are combined, they can result in tooth erosion, hiatal hernia, braded esophagus, kidney failure, osteoporosis, and death (Wolf, 1991).

Compulsive over-eaters mistake food for love. They can never make up for the love that was lacking in childhood, and they can never get enough food. Compulsive behavior at its most fundamental is a lack of self-love.

Self-destructive, compulsive behaviors are an expression of a belief for the sufferers that they are not good enough, or can be loved, as themselves. To a compulsive over-eater, anorexic or bulimic, the primary relationship is with food. In alcoholism or drug addiction, the primary relationship is with the drug of choice. With love addiction, the primary relationship is the fantasy of finding The Magic One. To the workaholic, the primary relationship is with work.

What all compulsive, addictive behaviors have in common is the detachment from a person that can supply them with real love and intimacy. Because they were previously emotionally abandoned, they reach for an illusion of love, a fantasy, or a drug to fulfill them. The substitution for the real thing soon becomes the instrument of their self-destruction.

IMPRINTING OF VIOLENCE

Self-destructive behaviors carry the element of unresolved grief. Child abuse and violent scenes are imprinted in the brain. They stay imprinted because they aren't grieved or integrated. These traumas usually get erased from conscious memory. They are too painful to remember. Later the child grows up and unconsciously acts out the earlier scenes. This is the beginning of the self-destructive, and revictimizing behavior.

Abused children repeat the cycle of violence and pass it down, one generation to another. When John Bradshaw aired his series, *The Family* on TV, he received 15,000 letters from prisoners describing their childhood abuse.

A victimized person never knows what may happen. Anyone can rape you, hit you, molest you or sexually harass you. You feel out of control, have no boundaries and little defense against the revictimization that ensues.

Your inner space has been violated. An incest victim may act out and go to bed with anyone. More than eighty-five percent of prostitutes were molested as children.

Addictions and compulsions cause the very thing the victim wishes to escape—the sadness, loss, grief, stress, and the out-of-control feeling. The addictions and compulsions, therefore compound the wreckage caused by the original abuse. The addictions and compulsions cause problems on multiple levels. When they are used as coping skills, for nourishment, for confidence, to bolster sagging self-esteem, to calm anxiety or to stop panic attacks, they wreak havoc.

Men who believe the myths that they must "know everything" and "act superior," often turn to alcohol to convince themselves that, in fact, they do know everything and are, indeed, invincible. Alcohol abuse is a factor in most of the violence against women.

Women, on the other hand, often take prescription drugs to suppress their depression, anxiety, fear and anger. By becoming dependent on drugs to modulated their moods, they deny themselves access to the very feelings that must be dealt with in order to learn how to protect themselves. The drugs further the victim process. Addictions and compulsions turn life into a disaster area.

But that's not all. People who become addicted stop maturing. If not already developmentally arrested due to childhood trauma, their maturation also stops at the level they are on when the addiction takes hold.

When a person stops maturing, emotions are frozen in time and place. That means a person may function on the emotional level of a four year old, while trying to cope as an adult in an adult world. This leads to *emotional reasoning*.

Emotional reasoning is part of immaturity. Using emotional reasoning, you make decisions based on how you *feel* rather than on logical deductions. You guess at answers to questions instead of finding out the facts. This type of imaginative thinking produces catastrophizing, poor judgement and self-destructive behavior. It creates additional feelings of helplessness and vulnerability.

You jump to conclusions instead of thinking through an idea to a logical deduction. For example, you think, "I feel bad. It must be the weather. I'll buy something new to wear to cheer me up." You then go out and charge five pairs of new shoes and don't think about it again.

When the bill comes you think, "I'm so stupid. Why didn't I think about my pay check when I was buying all this." You berate yourself with your internal dialogue, and your self-esteem sinks lower. You feel worse, blame it on an upset stomach, and take a drink or pill to feel better. Again, you end up feeling worse. That's the typical effect of self-destructive behavior. You do it to feel better, but you end up feeling even worse than when you started. The cause and effect of self-destructive behaviors are often overlooked.

If you are engaged in some form of self-destructive behavior, trace the series of events back to the place where it originally started. Learn to identify the patterns of cause and effect. Then project the logical outcomes of future behavior by anticipating the consequences of your actions. In this way, you will correct a major deficit in your judgement and learn to avoid much pain and suffering.

SELF ABUSE

In the absence of an abuser, a person who habitually plays the *victim role* may revictimize herself through *learned helplessness*. She refuses to take responsibility for herself. She sees herself as helpless and vulnerable, controlled by mystical and/or outside forces—whether they are other people, her own internal instability or her own projections of looming disaster.

Unable to see herself as having any control over her life, the professional victim may try to protect herself by dissociating from reality. By doing this, she makes herself vulnerable to anyone who might choose to take advantage of her. One client remarked that she had an incredible feeling of personal power when she first realized she could control her own life. She learned to stop dissociating and stay in reality once she felt "safe."

Until a person gets to this point, she may try and end the internal pain, anger, fear, guilt, and feelings of worthlessness by trying to kill herself. Seeing herself as helpless, thinking there is nothing she can do that will change the way she feels, she may attempt suicide to find relief in death.

Conversely, she may jab at herself with scissors or a knife, not to kill herself, but to put the pain on the outside of herself. The cutting and bleeding stop the inner pain and externalize it. Endorphins, triggered by the brain, stop the pain and allow for a temporary reprieve. Since she feels relief, the behavior is rewarded and, therefore, repeated.

Self-destructive behavior may also be motivated by a desire to punish herself for the internal guilt she feels or for feelings of unworthiness. She may punish herself by sabotaging her success, her relationships, or her career. For example, she thinks, "I don't deserve a promotion, because I'm unworthy, tainted, etc." Then she starts coming late to work.

Relief comes as she sabotages herself. The internal need for punishment (atonement for the guilt) is temporarily satisfied—until the torment resurfaces once more. The punishment is like throwing a bone to a hungry, howling, dog. The bone is chewed for awhile and in a short time the dog is howling again.

Most self-destructive behavior initially brings some relief (secondary gains). Stress reducers such as drinking, spending sprees, or the relief from guilt by defeating oneself are repeated over and over. The desired relief lessens as each stress reducer becomes overused. As the amount of relief decreases, the behavior increases hoping to once again bring relief. Eventually the behavior becomes addictive.

Addictive and compulsive behaviors never bring full or absolute relief from the gnawing inner emptiness. Self-destructive behaviors only serve to disguise and deny the pain. They never address the real problem: the inability to recover, accept, love and integrate, the missing parts of the self.

Chapter Thirteen

Personality Fragmentation

When Vickie came to therapy, she had multiple problems: binge eating and purging, love addiction, compulsive exercising, perfectionism— you name it, she had it. She had been in therapy off and on most of her adult life. She had even attended a sexual abuse treatment program recommended by a former therapist.

"I don't actually remember any sexual abuse," Vickie said, "but I sure didn't get this crazy all by myself." The sexual abuse program had helped her get in touch with some of her feelings, but she still had large, blank spaces in her memory. She couldn't remember any of her high school years, even though she was elected the most popular in her senior class.

She had married her high school sweetheart soon after high school graduation. He was physically, emotionally and verbally abusive. The marriage ended in divorce several years and two children later. He had Vickie committed by a "kangaroo court" to a mental institution in an effort to humiliate her for leaving and to gain custody of the children. Vickie was given labels by many doctors paid for by her husband. The labels left her confused and feeling she was crazy.

The court battles went on for years. At her husband's insistence, she submitted to multiple psychological tests to prove her fitness as a mother. The children would be given to their father at one hearing and to their mother at the next. They were pulled back and forth until, finally, Vickie thought it would be better for them to stay with their father. She sacrificed her motherhood to remove her children from the tug of war.

Vickie remarried, but it only lasted a short time. She had a succession of short term relationships, but none materialized into the dream of divine love she envisioned. She had a pattern of falling instantly in love, only to find the object of her affection fleeing from her or draining her dry.

It was her inability to sustain a healthy relationship that brought her to therapy. She fell in love with a man who wouldn't work, took her money, and spent his time drinking and doing drugs. He combed her hair and told her bedtime stories, thereby making her feel special.

It would have been obvious to the most casual observer that

Vickie had a great deal of anger at men, although she was largely unaware of it. She often amused herself, and sometimes others, by saying that the most useful purpose for men's penises was to slice them up and use them for "peckaroni pizza."

During her therapy sessions, Vickie learned to associate the emotional deprivation and abuse in her childhood with an anger at men and with her inability to have a healthy relationship. In one session she would be totally optimistic about her future, and in the next, so depressed she wanted to kill herself or the man with whom she was currently in love.

Vickie had multiple and diverse talents. She could sew and design clothes and had actually supported herself at one time by doing this. She was an accomplished artist and writer and could also do accounting and legal secretary work.

She also had an unusual talent for predicting the future and seeing into the past. During her childhood, she had developed the ability to predict when the next abuse might occur and, therefore, avoid it. She had learned to carefully observe the people in her environment. In this way, she could protect herself by accurately determining what kinds of things others might do or say. She developed a "psychic connection." Eventually, she fine-honed this skill and went into business for herself as a psychic. She developed a successful and large following.

No description of Vickie's talents is complete without mention of her striking beauty. Her friends and acquaintances often remarked about her pale peach complexion, long blonde hair, and dark eyes that seemed to penetrate right through to their souls.

The signs of personality fragmentation were also there. Each one of Vickie's aspects—the psychic, the workaholic, Miss Congeniality, the artist, the dress designer, the writer, the love addict, the angry one, the accountant—had taken on a life of its own. As the events of her sexual abuse were uncovered and worked through, the different personality fragments became known and integrated. Vickie found the angry part of herself during an inner child visualization. She had named this inner child Ramboette, as the image was dressed as a warrior, wearing guns, boots and hand grenades. Ramboette stood on barren, seared earth with an angry red sky all about her. She was ready to attack anyone and everyone.

Ramboette looked at Vickie. "Why don't you acknowledge me? I'm going to tell what happened," she said. When Vickie did acknowledge her, the headaches she had suffered for years went away. Vickie taught Ramboette how to be assertive, not aggressive, as well as the appropriate ways of setting limits with others and how to deal with her anger.

Soon after Ramboette was recovered, another child emerged as a black blob. The black blob was her helpless, weak, shy and needy child. Vickie didn't want anything to do with her because the child had been sexually abused.

Vickie painted a picture of the black blob. She used the picture to further get in touch with the blob's pain and helplessness, and to understand its neediness. Finally, she was able to accept the blob as a hurt inner child. "The child couldn't defend herself. It wasn't her fault she was sexually abused, although at first, that's the way it felt. It's like that poor child was a kitten that got eaten. It's not the kitten's fault it got eaten because it was weak and helpless," Vickie cried with compassion. Ramboette took the frightened and shy, needy inner child to protect and help her mature. She named her Shawna. All the different aspects of Vickie learned to communicate with Shawna and to integrate her talents and abilities.

This was accomplished through hypnosis, inner child work, and other methods described later in this book. Her eating disorder and her other compulsive behaviors of perfectionism, exercise, workaholic tendencies and love addiction, abated as she learned to meet her own needs, and stop compulsively meeting the needs of others.

• • •

Personality fragmentation occurs as a result of extreme child abuse (such as incest), where caretakers who are supposed to love the child, betray and use her for their own selfish needs. The personality shatters like a broken mirror; the victimized child cannot cope with the pain.

Some fragments hold the pain and the memory of the abuse, while others construct a new personality amnesic to it. The new personalities are designed as defensive maneuvers to protect the survivor, but may end up defeating her instead.

One personality fragment often mirrors the abusive perpetrator. It has contempt for the survivor because she was helpless, weak, and abused. The survivor thinks it is her fault she was betrayed, and judges herself worthless—worth less—and, therefore, deserving of punishment.

This part of the survivor identifies with the aggressor. It says, "It is not I who am overwhelmed and powerless, for I am the one doing the punishing."

Its job is to punish the survivor and continue to persecute her, just as the perpetrator did. With less severe fragmentation, the perpetrator is interjected into the personality as internal dialogue—the thoughts that go over and over in the mind—talking in the same manner as did the perpetrator.

Other personality fragments are designed to protect the victim by holding and denying anger or pain so as to remove the memory of the unbearable. Fragmentation allows the child to survive in a hostile environment by protecting herself with a new personality—to help her function in an abusive world.

If you think about maturational stages as evolutionary, it is easier to understand the how and why of personality fragmentation. Imagine, for example, that the brain has several distinct regions that continue developing after birth. Each region has an internal blueprint for when it "opens" and can be developed.

The first one to open, some have named the "fish stem" brain. It controls the basic instincts. Physical signs of the fish stem brain include the lack of blink response and the tongue going side to side. This is called the "reptile effect." At the age of four, this region is sealed and no new input can be imposed on the blueprint.

Children who do not learn to cross crawl, or whom experience trauma during this time, frequently do not get all the neuro-connections made in their brains, and may develop learning disabilities as a result.

If the trauma is severe, the newly developing personality may fragment and become isolated in this region of the brain. It is "frozen" at the time the trauma takes place and most often is that of a frightened, clinging young child, who is concerned mainly with survival.

The next brain blueprint to unfold has been called the midbrain or the "mammalian" brain. This deals mainly with emotions and the lymphatic system. Long term habits are stored in this region and are chemically operated. This region's blueprints are filled in until the age of seven, and then closed to new information. If a child is between the ages of four to seven when severe trauma takes place, the personality fragments in this region, and development is arrested. The result is an emotionally liable, unstable, personality.

The next stage in the evolution begins at age seven and ends at age eleven. The imaginary blueprint for the left hemisphere is unfolding during this time for imprinting. If the personality is fragmented during these years, the personality is developmentally arrested in the left hemisphere. The resulting personality fragment is cold and intellectual.

The last stage of childhood evolution begins at age eleven and ends at about the age of twenty-one, when the right hemisphere opens for imprinting. Personality fragmentation during this time results in a developmentally arrested, spaced out, eternal, adolescent. The head is in the clouds and the person may be distracted many times on the way to the grocery store or may find it difficult to balance a check book. She may use *emotional reasoning* when making decisions.

In the case of multiple traumas at various ages, personality fragmentation may occur in all the different regions. Without treatment, the personality fragments may not communicate among themselves, or even know about the existence of the others. One personality fragment may try and kill off another, not realizing they all inhabit the same body. Or they may be heard talking among themselves inside the head, making the victim feel crazy.

Each fragment may think it is the only one. The person is left confused. As the personality fragments compete with each other for body time, the person may experience missing gaps of time in her experience.

When the personality is fragmented, the person feels unstable and out of control. She never knows what she's going to be thinking or doing from one moment to the next. Depression is an almost universal symptom in a person who has personality fragmentation.

When a stressful situation arises, the different personalities may switch from one to another in rapid succession, as in a hot potato game, each trying to avoid the stress. This switching compensates the person to such an extreme degree that she may be unable to protect herself during a crisis. Many women with fragmented personalities become rape victims. Normally, switching takes place several times a day, as the personality fragments compete for body time. This causes disorientation and lack of continuity of experience.

Moods shift with the switches, and the focus of attention and concentration are lost each time. The victim blames it on a poor memory because she can't remember what's happened or she fails to get things accomplished.

The most common picture of a person who is struggling with personality fragmentation is someone who:
- is depressed
- is depleted
- is extremely intelligent, creative and likable
- is very anxious
- has severe headaches
- has amnesic episodes
- makes suicidal attempts
- engages in self-mutilation
- uses alcohol and drugs to control or cover dissociative experiences and decrease psychic pain
- has nightmares
- has sleep disturbances
- has phobias
- has somatic complaints (especially gastrointestinal and gynecological symptoms)
- has a wide range of sexual difficulties since most (80%) have been sexually abused
- feels unstable because she can't count on herself

This range of symptoms produces a person who feels like a

victim all the time. She does not know what to expect from herself. Take the example of a multi-talented, but fragmented individual. She starts one project, such as a painting, then a switch occurs, and now she's housecleaning. She forgets the painting, only to be later distracted by yet another interest or mood (fragment). It may be a week before she sits down to her easel to paint again. She berates herself for not having finished it the first time. These individuals have a hard time finishing what they start when their attention is changed by fragment switches.

One way to compensate for the switches is to carry a notebook at all times. Write down your intentions and refer to the notebook off and on during the day. Before you go to bed at night, make lists of what you want to accomplish the next day. Refer to the list often so you can remember what you started out to do.

Most of the time, what passes for self-destructive behavior is actually an attempt to protect the victimized child. For example, a suicide attempt may be one of the personality fragments trying to kill off another fragment, perhaps the "persecutor."

Another scenario is where the part that is responsible for holding anger may not be able to contain it any longer. It explodes like a volcano, leaving the unsuspecting victim shocked, embarrassed and unable to understand what happened—and sometimes out of a job.

Or when the victim senses her angry feelings and fears she might explode, she may start drinking or taking drugs, trying to suppress or regulate her angry feelings and to stabilize her emotions.

Due to all the internal conflicts, headaches are a common symptom of this disorder. Prescription drugs may be abused, simply trying to numb the pain, but lead to addiction. When the pain becomes unbearable, the sufferer may go on a buying spree, trying to feel better.

When there is a great deal of conflict between the personality fragments, and little communication among them, a person may experience time lapses. The different personality fragments may fight among themselves to take control of the body. If the fragments will communicate among themselves, they can usually arrange a system whereby the person can function. For instance, one fragment can be responsible for working and earning a living, while another is responsible for going to school. Still another can take care of the social functioning and relationships.

The part that was responsible for persecuting the sufferer, can be redefined to be in charge of protecting the person from harm. This cooperation will improve the overall functioning of the afflicted person. The agreements as to how the fragments can all get along and have their needs met eventually leads to integration and a unified whole personality.

Even though it may initially make a person feel "weird," encouraging the fragments to communicate among themselves and find areas of commonality helps the healing process. The ability to tolerate hearing the voices in the head until all the different personality fragments can achieve final integration is important. The assistance of a therapist is highly recommended in the working through, and integration of, personality fragments.

Taking medication to get rid of the voices is useless and counterproductive. What is necessary for integration, is for each one of the fragments to be singled out, and its memories retrieved and shared with all the other parts of the personality. As long as the fragments are living a life of their own, they can exert an influence upon self-destructive behavior. Inner child work is one method that produces excellent results for investigating the trauma, sharing memories, and final integration.

While the Multiple Personality Disorder, now renamed Dissociative Identity Disorder, is supposedly rare, more and more cases are being reported. As the subject of child abuse has come out of the closet, most therapists now understand how to identify and treat the identity disorder.

The degree of personality fragmentation depends on the age of the child when the trauma occurred and the severity of the abuse. Most abuse victims experience some personality fragmentation.

Occasionally, some therapists hesitate to tell their clients they have such a disorder; because their clients, desperate for an identity, may latch onto the label instead of working through and resolving the disorder. Labeling is a source of conflict among many therapists who think the labels are unnecessary—except for insurance purposes—as clients in therapy are constantly changing and developing.

METHODS OF INTEGRATION

There are numerous methods of retrieval and integration of personality fragments. One is hypnosis, which requires the assistance of a therapist, another is meditation, still another is the inner child work described in Chapter Fourteen.

In this chapter, several methods will be discussed: 1) Jean Houston's Prolepsis, 2) reframing, 3) two hands integrative method, and 4) Virginia Satir's Parts Party. Each will involve a creative visualization, to enable the various fragments, isolated in different "brains," to communicate with each other. All four of the integrative methods may be used at the same time or they may be used separately. All help achieve an integration of the parts into a whole.

The subconscious mind loves novelty and variety. It is very curious to find new ways to operate. Once you see and understand how to integrate the personality fragments, free your imagination to think of your own creative visualizations. Follow through with what you start. Write down your process, and be sure to journal your results. Refer to your journal recordings frequently to see the new emerging patterns in your personality. Also note the new behaviors and your reactions to them.

Creative visualization for connecting fragments

Creative visualization is an easy method that helps the different fragments learn to communicate with each other. For this exercise, I will refer back to the "brain regions" in which fragments are isolated.

Allow your body to relax and go to your *safe place*. With eyes closed, imagine you are looking back into the "fish stem" in your brain. It is located toward the base of your neck. Roll your eyes that way—as far back to the base of your neck as possible.

Then create or imagine you are constructing a super highway going toward your midbrain or "mammalian" brain located in the center of your head. Follow the highway with your eyes as it connects these two sections. Do this several times.

Next, continue to visualize building the highway from this center part into the left hemisphere of your brain. Trace it with your eyes several times. Continue to visualize constructing the highway to connect the left hemisphere with the right hemisphere. Trace it with your eyes several times.

Then connect all the regions together by visualizing highways into each one of them so that they may exchange information. Trace the highways with your eyes to show the regions the new highways of communication. Tell each brain region to communicate its information with the other regions.

You may want to repeat this exercise one week apart for six weeks. Be sure to give yourself a reward each time you do this exercise. Positive reinforcement helps.

Jean Houston's Prolepsis

I learned this technique at Jean Houston's seminars. It is called Prolepsis, and it attempts to harvest who you were in evolution in order that you can become who you might be as you continue to evolve. In so doing, it helps the different regions in which fragments are stored to integrate experiences and expand beyond their isolation by reenacting the developmental stages from fish to human. This technique was done in a group, but it can just as easily be done on an individual basis using the following instructions. It is best when appropriate music is played.

Remove your shoes, glasses, belts, jewelry, and anything that you may be wearing that would inhibit free movement. Lie flat on your stomach, your arms at either side, and gently roll from side to side.

Make sure that your body rolls as a single unit, torso and lower body not differentiated from each other. This is the stage of the fish and corresponds to the rolling stage of early infancy. Do this for five minutes.

You are now evolving into an amphibian. Begin crawling along on your forearms dragging your tail (your lower body) along. This stage and movement corresponds to the period in which the infant is beginning to pull itself along on its forearms.

If you get tired, stop and continue the movement with your senses until you are rested enough to continue it physically. Allow your mind to be open to an awareness of amphibian life and experience (five minutes).

Next comes the reptile stage, where you will experience much greater use and coordination of the legs with your arms. For the most part, you are still crawling on your belly but you are land-bound now and have greater capacity for locomotion. Your arms and legs carry you more easily from one place to another.

When you make these movements, you are activating the

parts of your brain memory that have to do with the infant's movements when it starts to crawl on its belly and has greater coordination of arms and legs. Let there rise in you an awareness and experience of reptilian life (five minutes).

The reptile evolves into an early mammal, capable of moving on all fours. This corresponds to the stage of the infant when it gets off its belly and walks on all fours. At this stage, the early mammal discovers its capacity to make sounds. Make the movements of the early mammal. By making these movements you are activating the "mammalian" region (five minutes).

Somewhere during the course of evolution these early mammals evolve into early little monkeys. Make the movements and the sounds of the early little monkeys and discover what it is to live in the bodies of these creatures. This corresponds to the period in the infant's life in which it stands up from time to time, as well as gains greater facility of movement. As you do this, you are activating your own memory. Live now the movements and experiences of the early little monkey (five minutes).

The early little monkeys evolve into the higher monkeys, corresponding to the great apes and gorillas. Become now a higher monkey making the appropriate movements and gestures. This is thought to relate to the child's acquiring greater strength and surety of movement, and the ability to swing from side to side. Let memories corresponding to this period of evolution be activated, as you experience the movements and experiences of the higher monkey (five minutes).

You are now becoming the early human being. Early humans were involved in a great deal of ingenious discovery, such as toolmaking. Their jaws were thrust forward, and their bodies more apelike than ours, but they were filled with a curiosity and an intelligence that moved them away from animal life into a whole new experience of being alive in the world. This stage corresponds to roughly the twenty-eighth to the thirty-sixth months of a child's life.

As you experience the early human, both male and female, let your mind be filled with the experiences of the reality that they may have encountered, and the struggles they may have known. Know that in doing this, your memory is being stimulated to recall the early stages of our lives as human beings (five minutes).

Gradually, the early human evolves into the present day human being. You have ten minutes to experience this physical and social evolution. Explore the various stages of speech and development, hunting, agriculture, building, exploration, religious development, political development, civilization, and industrialization, until you arrive at the present era.

In ten minutes, go through as many of these as you can, and in your enactment of the evolutionary journey, recall in both your body and mind as many of these stages as possible. This corresponds to the development of a child from three years old to maturity.

Now become the next stage in human evolution—the extended, evolved, human being. Discover with movement, body, voice, sound, gesture, contact and communication, what this stage might be like. If you wish to dance, sing, or make music, that is fine. Allow yourself a range of exploration into the nature and being-ness of the possible human (seven to ten minutes).

If you do this exercise alone, now is the time to write creatively, and wherever desired, draw pictures of this experience in your journal. If you do this with other people, pair up and lie on the floor with your heads together, and tell each other of your experiences. Say to each other, "Tell me what you remember about being a fish." Beginning with, "I am a fish . . ." let the memories and images pour out from each of you in dialogue.

Do not worry where they come from. Just let these images and memories rise spontaneously, and communicate or write them down as freely as you can. Do this for each stage you went through: fish, amphibian, reptile, early mammal, early monkey, higher monkey, early human, human being, and finally the memories of the extended human being. In so doing, you are connecting, integrating and giving meaning to all the various areas of your past which are stored in your brain as memories.

Reframing

Most self-destructive behavior has secondary gains. Secondary gains can include evading responsibility for acting out behavior, because you can't remember doing it. Another type of secondary gain is the useful part of the destructive behavior, such as relieving stress by drinking, or feeling less depressed by buying something new.

The reframing method addresses this need directly. It offers other, more useful, ways to meet the secondary gains and eliminates self-destructive behavior. Sometimes self-destructive behavior is simply the result of a stress related habit such as drinking. You may have reduced the stress, yet continue doing it because it has become addictive and a part of you. Habits usually take three weeks to break.

Another cause of self-destructive behavior is where the victim has been made to feel as if she is a "bad" person. She may do bad things because she thinks and feels she is "bad." In this sense, she's protecting her identity.

Self-destructive behavior often strives in distorted ways to protect the victim. By finding new and more creative ways to meet the positive intent of the self-destructive behavior, much of the undesirable quality of the behavior can be eliminated.

Very often, the subconscious personality fragments are very

childlike and concrete in their reasoning for doing things the way they do. Sometimes just making the effort of communicating with them is all it takes for them to mature and engage in a positive frame of mind.

There are six steps in reframing.
1. Identify the unwanted behavior you wish to change. The behavior may be anything you wish to change to a positive intent. It can include compulsive eating, the drinking personality, the part that's responsible for compulsive spending, the perfectionistic part, etc.

2. In a relaxed state of mind, with your feet flat on the floor and your hands resting on the arms of the chair or by your side, say to yourself, "Would the part of me that is responsible for causing me to _____ (eat compulsively, etc.) please give me a signal in reality by an honest, unconscious movement of my right forefinger (you may also use other body signals).

   Touch your right forefinger with another finger to indicate to your subconscious the part of the body you are talking about. Pay attention to any sound, picture, feeling, or thought you might get. You will receive some type of signal. This process begins the building of a bridge between your conscious mind and the subconscious, so that you can communicate with it using these signals.

   Designate the unconscious movement of the right forefinger to signal a "yes" answer, and the left forefinger to signal a "no" answer. Do this by slightly touching the right and left forefingers as you give the instructions. If the

body chooses another signal, then have a "yes" answer as a louder sound or brighter picture or a stronger feeling. A "no" answer would be a diminishing of the signal.
When the signal comes, again ask the part that you're trying to contact, if you received the signal it intended. Request it to intensify the signal so you can be sure you are communicating with it. When you receive the intensified signal, you are ready to go on to the next step. If you have a therapist, the therapist watches for any noticeable behavioral response of which you may be unaware.

3. The next step is to separate the intention from the behavior. Once the part of you that's responsible for the behavior is in communication with you, ask "What is the purpose of _____(the undesirable behavior)?

Most often, the answer is, "I'm trying to protect you." Sometimes the answer will seem to be an undesirable intention, such as, "I'm trying to kill you" or "you don't deserve success because you're worthless." When this happens, take another step back by asking, "What are you trying to do for me by killing me?" "What do you think makes me worthless?" This allows you to obtain a more useful answer, such as "I'm trying to keep you from being abused" or, "I'm trying to save you from this miserable life" or, "because you were abused."

If you receive the latter answer, explain that you were not the cause of the abuse, and ask that part to be the protector to keep you from being abused in the future. Do not send it to the creative part to design better ways to abuse you. A basic part of reframing is plain common sense.

4. The fourth step involves asking the part that is responsible for the undesirable behavior to go to the creative part. Ask the creative part to develop ten new, more satisfying behaviors to protect you or help you other than what is currently being done. Tell your creative part to be wildly creative in developing the new ways of being. Ask it to give you a finger signal on your right forefinger each time it develops a new behavior.

When the ten new behaviors have been developed, ask all the parts of the brain to look and examine the appropriateness of the new behaviors. Ask if any parts have any objections to the behaviors. Have them designate a "no" signal on your left forefinger if there are any objections. If there are no objections, then have them give a "yes" signal on the right forefinger.

If there are objections, you may request for those behaviors to be deleted, or reframe the objections. Using the before mentioned communication signals, ask if there are at least three acceptable new behaviors. If there aren't, go back to the first step and go through the process until you have at least three new and better behaviors. When this is accomplished, go on to step 5.

5. Have the originally identified part accept the new choices and take responsibility for generating them when needed. Ask the original part if it agrees that the new choices are at least as effective as the original, unwanted behavior. If it says "yes" (using the preestablished mode of communication to insure continuity), ask if it is willing to accept responsibility for generating three new behaviors in the

appropriate contexts. It is usually glad to accept the new role.

6. For the final step, ask the part that is now responsible for generating the new behaviors, to imagine a time in the future when they will be needed. Allow the part to go through a "dry run" several times to practice how to initiate and install the new behaviors. When this is accomplished, the reframing is completed.

Two hands integrative method

The two hands integrative method is another way of helping conflicted aspects of the personality become cohesive. Using this method, hold your two hands palm up in front of you.

Visualize a part of you in one hand. For example, if there is a compulsive eating problem, or other self-destructive behavior, visualize that aspect of you in one hand. Imagine a color on the visualization. Allow the color to come to your mind.

In the other hand, visualize the other part of you, such as the protector part that's looking out for your best self-interests. Select a color from your imagination and put it on that visualization. Make sure the healthier one is equally strong, or stronger, than the self-destructive one. You can make it stronger by adding more positive aspects to it, such as combining several different positive aspects together.

Feel the weight of both hands. Is one heavier than the other? Does one feel rough and the other smooth? Notice the differences between them. Hear the sounds each makes, smell their smells, and visualize the aspects in every way. Make the images as complete as possible. Have the two parts talk to each other, holding your hands with the images close together. Find out what their purposes, differences and similarities are.

Eventually, request them to merge together. Sometimes the different aspects think they are complete and independent as they are and don't want to. Each one thinks the body belongs to it. They are often very childlike with limited reasoning capabilities. In a kind and loving way, explain the reality of the situation and that they will all be stronger if they combine forces. Sometimes, this alone is enough for differing aspects to join together.

If they refuse to unite, have them communicate more. Use problem solving skills to work out the differences until they do agree to join forces. Then mix the two colors from your hands together. As they blend, the integration takes place.

Even if resistance is there, it can usually be overcome. With the representation of the aspects fully developed in both palms, very slowly clasp the hands together. This can result in fusion. When the full integration of the colors is achieved, fold the images from both hands back into your heart area and feel the warmth enter your body as wholeness takes place.

Virginia Satir's Parts Party

The parts party method requires a relaxed, meditative state of mind with the eyes closed. When you are comfortable and relaxed, go to your *safe place*. Visualize a large table, with six or seven seats around it. Then ask for six or seven of the personality fragments to each sit in a different seat.

Go around the table, and allow each one to tell you who they are, how old each one is, and anything else they might want to talk about. If one is very young and frightened, ask one of the older and more knowledgeable protector types to assist the younger one and help it mature.

Allow them to communicate among themselves, encouraging them to settle differences and conflicts peacefully by negotiating with one another. Treat them all as equals. When you wish to end the parts party, thank them all for coming and sharing with one another.

This technique can be repeated over and over. There may be different parts at each subsequent meeting, or they may change over time to more mature and sophisticated parts. As their differences are settled, they may eventually integrate on their own.

Chapter Fourteen

Posttraumatic
Stress Disorder

Posttraumatic stress disorder occurs after a sudden, unexpected, shocking event or series of blows assaults you, such as in childhood sexual abuse, domestic violence, rape, traffic accidents, witnessing sudden death, and war-time stress. You probably won't become fully traumatized unless you feel utterly helpless and powerless during the incident or situations.

LOSS OF SELF

Loss of the sense of self happens when you are permanently changed by traumatic incidents such as childhood abuse, rape or domestic violence.

You still live with your remembrances of an old, normally functioning self. You may not remember a traumatic experience due to repression, but have constant fear, anxiety, and panic attacks. Or, if you do remember it, you may try not to think about the trauma.

This is a common defense, but the more you suppress it, the more flashbacks you'll have. You need to talk about it, and relive it through hypnosis or a relaxed state of consciousness as often as necessary to integrate it. Visualize a different outcome to the trauma. Visualize, for example, the offender behind bars or you fighting back successfully. Grieve the loss of your former life because a part of you that viewed the world as a *safe place* to live has died. A new world view must now be reconstructed.

The effects of childhood trauma can be found in attitudes and fears which persist into adulthood: long-standing superstitions, fascinations with horror books and movies, and fear of fear. Childhood traumas do not "fade away" as once thought.

Frequently, people with childhood traumas reenact them later in adult life. This tendency to master the trauma by recreating it may, in fact, lead to adult victimizations. Look for the patterns of victimization in your life and trace them back to your original trauma.

If you uncover a traumatic experience from your childhood, it's best to talk it out with a non-judgmental friend or therapist. Be sure and go at your own pace and construct an internal *safe place* (described later in this chapter) before processing the trauma. If you try to do too much, too fast, you may become overwhelmed and retraumatize yourself.

Full recovery may take years. As you develop the ability to cope with the situation by talking it out, the trauma may resolve itself. Don't force anything. Allow the healing to take place naturally. Like mending a wounded heart, to promote healing, give yourself the nurturing, love, and understanding you needed at the time you were traumatized. Reassure yourself daily that you are healing and becoming whole.

Because of the extreme pressure and stress caused by a Posttraumatic Stress Disorder, many of the vitamins and minerals in your body may be leached out. Watch your diet, and make sure it's loaded with nutrients. Allow yourself extra rest, relaxation, and exercise, to help your body rebuild and become healthy and strong again. A vacation or break in your routine may be helpful.

DSM IV

The American Psychiatric Association: *Diagnostic and Statistical Manual of Mental Disorders*, Fourth Edition, commonly known as the DSM IV, gives the following criteria for Posttraumatic Stress Disorder.

A. The person has been exposed to a traumatic event in which both of the following were present:

(1) the person experienced, witnessed, or was confronted with an event or events that involved actual or threatened death or serious injury, or a threat to the physical integrity of self or others

(2) the person's response involved intense fear, helplessness, or horror. Note: In children, this may be expressed instead by disorganized or agitated behavior

B. The traumatic event is persistently reexperienced in one (or more) of the following ways:

(1) recurrent and intrusive distressing recollections of the event, including images, thoughts, or perceptions. Note: In young children, repetitive play may occur in which themes or aspects of the trauma are expressed.

(2) recurrent distressing dreams of the event. Note: In children, there may be frightening dreams without recognizable content.

(3) acting or feeling as if the traumatic event were recurring (includes a sense of reliving the experience, illusions, hallucinations, and dissociative flashback episodes, including those that occur on awakening or when intoxicated.) Note: In young children trauma-specific reenactment may occur.

(4) intense psychological distress at exposure to internal or external cues that symbolize or resemble an aspect of the traumatic event

(5) physiological reactivity on exposure to internal or external cues that symbolize or resemble an aspect of the traumatic event

C. Persistent avoidance of stimuli associated with the trauma and numbing of general responsiveness (not present before the trauma), as indicated by three (or more) of the following:

(1) efforts to avoid thoughts, feelings, or conversations associated with the trauma

(2) efforts to avoid activities, places, or people that arouse recollections of the trauma

(3) inability to recall an important aspect of the trauma

(4) markedly diminished interest or participation in significant activities

(5) feeling of detachment or estrangement from others

(6) restricted range of affect (e.g., unable to have loving feelings)

(7) sense of a foreshortened future (e.g. does not expect to have a career, marriage, children, or a normal life span)

D. Persistent symptoms of increased arousal (not present before the trauma), as indicated by two (or more) of the following:

(1) difficulty falling or staying asleep
(2) irritability or outbursts of anger
(3) difficulty concentrating
(4) hypervigilance
(5) exaggerated startle response

E. Duration of the disturbance (symptoms in B, C, and D) is more than 1 month

F. The disturbance causes clinically significant distress or impairment in social, occupation, or other important areas of functioning.

ABNORMAL BRAIN WAVES

The emotional recovery from Posttraumatic Stress Disorder is complicated by other problems. Brain rhythms, the electrical impulses associated with states of attention and consciousness, become abnormal. They are popularly called "brain waves" because they are recorded as "waves" on graph paper (the electroencephalographic record or EEG).

There are four major brain rhythms. The beta rhythm is associated with active thinking or active attention. In beta, the attention is focused on the external world or problem solving.

The alpha rhythm is associated with a relaxed, internally focused state with closed eyes. The mind is alert but at ease and not focused on external processes or engaged in organized, analytical, or problem-solving thinking. It's the state of mind you pass through as you drift to sleep and as you wake up.

The theta rhythm is usually associated with drowsy or semi-unconscious states. It appears as consciousness slips toward unawareness. It is often accompanied by hypnagogic (dream like) images. The delta rhythm is primarily associated with deep sleep.

When you have a Posttraumatic Stress Disorder, you're vigilant. The alpha brain waves become diminished and produce waves of poor quality. You can't relax or drift off to sleep. When you do sleep, it's light and you frequently jerk awake. Your attention is riveted on the external world, scanning for the next danger or attack, either real or imagined. Your senses are hyper-alert. The immune and digestive systems become depressed. As the body's stored up supplies of energy are depleted, stress and fatigue set in.

Continuous stress causes chemical changes in the body. The brain's neurotransmitters become inoperable or inefficient and the natural opiates for fighting pain and stresses become overtaxed. That means you can't concentrate and frequently forget what's on your mind. You may develop a craving for food, drugs or alcohol to relieve the stress. A deep depression usually sets in.

Once you learn to feel safe again and relax your body and mind, you can start healing. But once the damage is done, it may take the neurotransmitters and bodily organs up to two years to recover.

A Posttraumatic Stress Disorder may lie dormant for years before it is triggered. Children with a Posttraumatic Stress Disorder may develop differently as a result of it; changes in neurotransmitters, hormones, and regulation of the autonomic nervous system have been reported.

Children as young as two years of age can have symptoms typical of Posttraumatic Stress Disorder; sleep disturbances, night terrors, intrusive memories and flashbacks, separation anxiety, aggressiveness and hyperactivity, emotional detachment, and constriction.

Anyone who has lived in a home where violence occurred,

anyone who has witnessed a violent crime or been a victim of one, and even patients who are unprepared for surgery are also subject to Posttraumatic Stress Disorder.

Extreme stress can cause a breakthrough into consciousness of repressed memories of childhood abuse and trigger Posttraumatic Stress Disorder and flashbacks. Relaxation can also causes flashbacks and breakthroughs in repressed memories. Ironically, at a time in your life where it calms down and everything seems to be going well—the unconscious may open repressed memories and trigger a delayed Posttraumatic Stress Disorder.

RELAXATION

An especially important part of overcoming a Posttraumatic Stress Disorder is to learn to relax completely. Proper breathing is an important aspect of relaxing. Watch a baby breathe from the abdomen. Babies are naturally relaxed. A simple test to determine where you're breathing is to place one hand on your chest and one hand on your abdomen. Which hand moves?

When anxious and fearful, people breathe high in their chest, causing reverse thoracic breathing. The brain constantly monitors the location of the diaphragm. When breathing is high in the chest, such as in reverse thoracic breathing, the brain receives a message of fear and sends chemical signals to the body to be hyper-vigilant and scan the environment for danger.

Learning to redirect the breath to deep, slow, diaphragmatic breathing helps to stop the hypervigilance and automatic scanning. If you've been doing reverse thoracic breathing, deep diaphragm breathing may feel strange. Remind yourself to pay attention to your breath, and redirect it in a kind, gentle manner, to slow down, and breathe from your diaphragm instead of your chest.

Deep relaxation helps reduce depression and chronic stress.

When you're anxious, the small vessels close off under the surface of the skin to provide an extra blood supply to the brain, heart, lungs, and large muscles. When this happens, the skin becomes cooler (because of the reduced blood flow). The sayings, "cold hands—warm heart," and "white as a sheet" refer to this response.

Relaxation is characterized by slow, deep breathing, slow heart rate, increased digestion, bowel and bladder function, unfocused mental activity and surface (skin) warming.

Relaxation changes blood flow. Since the brain, heart, lungs, and large muscles have a decreased oxygen demand, the blood supply is reduced to those body parts, and can return to the surface areas and the digestive tract.

Relaxation can be accomplished in five or six sessions of thirty minutes twice a day, or forty-five minute sessions four times a week. There are several different methods of relaxation depending on the severity of stress that is in the body. The simplest of the relaxation techniques is to tell your various body parts to relax and be calm and quiet. To begin relaxation training, find a comfortable position and relax your body as much as you can. Be aware of any remaining tension in your muscles and do what you need to completely relax those muscles. Now that you are relaxed, take five full deep breaths, and then breathe deeply and evenly from your abdomen. Make the in and out breath even and continuous. Do this for several breaths.

Now, on the next breath, as you exhale, close your eyes, and mentally see and repeat the number 3, three times. Trace it, each time, in your mind. On the next breath, see and repeat the number 2, three times. Trace it in your mind. Now see and repeat the number 1, three times on the next breath, and trace it in your mind, three times.

You will experience changes that are associated with relaxation. Deepen those experiences by slowly counting down from ten to one as you exhale each breath: ten, nine, eight, *deeper*, seven, six *calmer and deeper*, five, four and three, *deeper and deeper*, two and one.

While you are in a relaxed state, make visual images of your body relaxed. Remember a time from the past when you were totally relaxed and at peace with yourself and your environment. Create that scene in vivid detail. If you can't remember a time when you were relaxed, visualize a time in the future and see yourself totally relaxed. Imagine what relaxation feels like.

Because the blood flows away from the extremities during hypervigilance and scanning the environment for danger, you might visualize your feet in buckets of warm water. Make your images as vivid and real as possible. Start with your feet. Say, *feet, relax. I feel my feet getting warmer and warmer.* Say, *ankles, relax.* Visualize the relaxation, and imagine what it feels like. Make it real with the power of your mind.

Take your time and move slowly up your body to your calves. Say, *calves, relax. Knees, relax. Thighs, relax.* Make visual images of each part relaxed. Next, go to your hands. Suggest they are getting warmer and warmer. Make visual images of warming mittens on your hands. Tell your fingers to relax.

Then continue to relax your forearms. Say, *forearms, relax. Upper arms, relax. Lower, back, relax. Mid back, relax. Shoulders, relax.* Say, *my shoulders are loose and limp. The relaxation is moving into my neck. Neck relax. My scalp is relaxing. I can feel the relaxation draining down into my face. My eyelids are heavy and relaxed.* Leave a little space between your teeth. Say, *jaw relax. Throat, relax.*

You can do this exercise at bedtime as a sleep aid. To drift off to sleep, exhale twice as long as you inhale for several breaths. That will cause you to feel tired and sleepy. Relaxation is progressive. Each day you do the exercises, you feel more relaxed.

This type of relaxation helps quiet your muscles and ease your tension. Many people record a tape of their own relaxation instructions and listen to it while they relax. Relaxation in itself will help calm your anxiety.

When the stress has become chronic, the muscles don't know how to relax and go into a state of contraction and are tight and tense all the time. They think tension is normal, so they strive to maintain a certain degree of tension. The muscles need retraining. Do this by flexing and relaxing the different muscle groups, so the muscles can learn the difference between tension and relaxation.

Start with your feet. Flex and relax them. Then take the muscle group from the ankles to the knee, and flex and relax them. Next, flex and relax the muscles from the knee to the hip. Flex and relax the hips. Flex and relax your hands, forearms and upper arms, one muscle group at a time. Flex and relax the muscles in the lower back, abdomen, chest, and then the upper back, shoulders, neck, scalp and face, one muscle group at a time.

In a deep state of relaxation, with your eyes closed, project your body onto a mental view screen. Scan your body, up and down, up and down, looking for signs of any remaining tension. Do what you need to completely and totally relax. If you image on your mental view screen, any dark or gray areas in your body, mentally project a golden healing light into those areas. Make it real with the power of your imagination.

You are in a deeper state of relaxation now. Continue the experience. Mentally repeat to yourself each of the following phrases three times:

I am relaxing . . . . . . .my body . . . . .completely
I feel heavy . . . . .and warm . . . . .all over
I am calm . . . . .peaceful . . . . .and serene

Repeat the following sentences slowly and with frequent pauses that relate to heaviness and warmth.

- *I am quite relaxed.*
- *My arms and hands feel heavy and warm.*
- *I feel calm and peaceful.*
- *My whole body is relaxed and my hands are warm.*
- *My hands are warm.*
- *Warmth is flowing into my hands, they are warm.*
- *My hands are warm, relaxed and warm.*

While you deepen the relaxation by making suggestions and visualizations of your hands and fingers getting warmer, your hand temperature rises. You get the best results when you have your hands close to your body.

People who have been traumatized usually have finger temperatures in the seventies. The object is to raise the temperature to ninety-six degrees for ten minutes or longer. This retrains the body to relax completely. A biofeedback temperature machine is an effective way of measuring your finger temperature.

SAFE PLACE

The next step in dispelling the impact of psychological trauma is to learn how to create a *safe place*. People who have been abused or traumatized don't have a place inside themselves where they feel safe. They're cut to the very heart of their soul. And because they feel hurt and betrayed, they won't trust others. This leads to isolation and loneliness.

You can create a *safe place* by following these simple instructions. Once you have taught your body to relax, focus your attention on the space between your eyebrows. Quiet the mind and body. Keep your muscles as still as possible. Take five fast, very deep, even breaths from the diaphragm. Then, on the exhalation of each breath after that, count consecutively from ten to one. On the first breath, think ten to yourself as you exhale. On the next breath, think nine as you exhale, and so on until you get to one.

Roll your eyes up as far as you can. Imagine you can look up through the top of your head. Then slowly lower your eyelids while you are looking up. After your eyes are closed, focus them on the spot between your eyebrows. Imagine your body is surrounded in an aura of impenetrable white light that is protecting you while you relax. When you feel relaxed, begin to image a room and decorate it with furniture. Paint or paper the walls, and do all the things to it you would do to a regular room. Hang pictures on the walls, and put a favorite chair in the room on which you can relax. Make it a place where you feel safe. Instead of a room, some people like to imagine a *safe place* in nature—a setting by a mountain lake or a sandy beach, for example.

Then see yourself, feel yourself, and hear yourself, relaxed in your *safe place*. Do this for at least twenty to thirty minutes each day. To deepen the relaxation, you may visualize walking on a beach or hiking in the mountains.

Impressions may appear in the form of feelings, or you may hear a voice or sounds. When images start to appear on their own, simply observe what happens without trying to analyze or think about it. Mentally focused activity brings you out of the deeper state of relaxation.

This is a process. Each day when you do this exercise, you'll relax a little deeper. It may take six or seven relaxation periods to relax deep enough to feel you're getting anywhere. Your conscious mind needs to relearn it's okay to let go and relax. When you do let go and relax, it becomes easier to relax all during the day.

As you relax, you may feel your body suddenly jerk and tense up again. Reassure yourself that you are safe. Eventually you will be able to stay relaxed. Your *safe place* will give you a sense of security and an inner resource upon which to draw peace and renewed strength. As you go very, very, deep into the relaxation, notice that you experience an objectivity about your body. You may see hypnagogic (dream like) images flash before you.

When this happens, the alpha waves are crossing over into theta waves. This is a state of deep relaxation, and necessary to achieve if the alpha waves are to return to normal. It's like pushing the reset button on a piece of machinery that's blown a fuse and stopped functioning. When you go into this deep state of relaxation, you're pushing the mental reset button so your body can normalize itself.

This crossover from alpha to theta brain wave activity is called *reverie*. The terminology used in describing the *reverie* state is called: the "fringe of consciousness," the "preconscious," the "transliminal mind," and "twilight state," to "transcendence."

If you will go into *reverie* thirty minutes a day, five days a week for six weeks, your stress level can lower and your body normalize. Your neuro-receptors may heal, and your brain waves return to normal. If you've used alcohol to help cope with your symptoms, stop drinking and allow the relaxation to work for you instead.

In the *reverie* state, you feel emotionally detached from whatever you see. Later, after you are out of *reverie* for about fifteen minutes, feelings of grief or sadness may surface and stay with you for several hours, days, or as long as it takes to dissolve that energy. You may have a dream that shows you a traumatic event or conflict. This is all part of the healing process.

Eventually your emotional conflicts will slowly surface for

you to deal with one at a time. Theoretically, the mind does not give you more than you can handle. You usually don't remember the trauma like it actually happened. One woman who recalled that she was sexually abused at age four, realized she had subsequently felt guilty and responsible for her abuse. Victims, especially children, often feel guilty and responsible for their own traumas. Another client, in reliving her rape, felt relieved and finally let it go.

Once you've relived your trauma, you'll probably feel relieved. It's what you repress that hurts you. Once you've remembered traumatic events, you'll probably stop repressing feelings because that's no longer necessary. This, in itself, is healing.

Any conflicts from your earliest childhood through adulthood may appear in hypnagogic (dream like) imagery. These images have been described as "more vivid," and "more realistic," than dreams, and they "come and go in a flash," and "contained detailed material which I didn't know I knew." The images may become foggy a session or two prior to the release of very sensitive, traumatic material. Seek a professional therapist or support system to help you process what comes up. It's important to talk about the experiences that have traumatized you in order to integrate them.

All memories, including traumatic repressed memories and childhood events are processed in the hippocampus region in the brain. This area has been referred to as a computer with "*write only*" programs. When you are in *reverie*, the door opens not only to read these "*write only*" programs but to rewrite them as well. After you are adept at achieving *reverie*, you may do advanced techniques to further your healing process. Doing inner child work while in *reverie* produces excellent healing results. *Reverie* can also be used to ask questions and receive answers, solve problems, receive inspiration, and develop creativity.

Going into *reverie* as a daily routine is known to enhance health and promote an overall sense of well-being. Obtaining *reverie* takes practice. The biggest challenge is to stay awake while you are in *reverie*. Ironically, falling asleep can also be an effort to avoid confrontation with your unconscious.

The chief thing to remember when doing deep relaxation is to *let go*. Do not become emotionally involved with what you see or feel, or try and figure out what the images mean.

As soon as you come out of *reverie*, write your impressions in your journal as fast as you can. Then process them. The hypnagogic (dream like) images are very fragile and quickly forgotten. Some people go so deep into *reverie* that they are disoriented when they come out of it. You may need to walk around for a few minutes until you get all the way back into beta brain waves. Until you feel stable, don't attempt to drive a car.

For maximum results, go into the *reverie* state of consciousness at least twenty to thirty minutes, five times a week, for six weeks. This will illicit the full healing process. The healing process involves not only retrieving lost memories but normalizing brainwave patterns and revitalizing brain neurotransmitters.

As you heal, you will notice an overall pattern of increased health and a heightened awareness of your surroundings. Colors will appear brighter, and sounds more vibrant and alive.

INNER CHILD VISUALIZATIONS

Even though you can't change the past, you can change how you feel about it. Reparenting your inner child can provide corrective emotional experiences. Aspects of your personality fragmented, due to emotional trauma or loss, can be healed and integrated. Inner child work, done over a period of a year or longer can help restructure your personality.

After you have processed the material from *reverie*, take a couple of deep breaths and again visualize your *safe place*. See yourself with all your adult strengths. Focus your awareness on any internal pain or fear you may feel. Picture those feelings as a hurt child. You might use an old photograph as a reminder. Go to your inner child and make friends (there may be several and they may be of either sex).

One client had five inner children, of differing ages and sexes. She had different names for each of them. However, even though each of them may have distinct characteristics, it is important to know that they are all aspects of you as a whole person. It is important to get them to cooperate together for integration even though they may not initially trust or like one another.

Tell your inner child you're here from the future, and assure your younger self that he or she survived. Ask your inner child to tell you about the fear or pain he or she feels. Visualize the traumatic event or events, then visualize the situation turning out differently. For instance, if there has been childhood abuse, talk back and refuse the advances of the perpetrator. Realize you have the ability to say "No" to an authority figure without fear of punishment or reprisal. You may want to visualize beating up the perpetrator or seeing him behind bars. If there is more than one inner child, encourage them to talk to each other and help each other.

Then tell your inner child you're going to protect him or her and make sure the trauma doesn't occur again. Hug the child and tell your younger self, he or she is loved and wanted. Ask, "What can I do to help you?" "What do you need from me at this time?" When you are finished reassuring your inner child, play with your inner child and have some fun. When you are ready to close the time with your inner child and return to outer reality, tell your inner child you will come back again.

Upon leaving, visualize your inner child in a *safe place*. Make an appointment for another time and be certain to keep it. Do not abandon your inner child and thereby recreate another rejection! You are in the process of creating a new life for yourself. Make it happen intentionally, not as an accident of whenever you might "think" or "feel like" doing inner child work. Once you start the process, keep it going. The energy builds up over time and becomes more and more powerful.

Writing letters to your inner child also helps. Use your dominant hand when you write to your inner child. Your inner child will answer by writing back with your non-dominant hand. You could also write a letter to your parents with your non-dominant hand, allowing the child in you to tell them all the things you needed from them but didn't get. It's not necessary to send it. Then start giving yourself those things you missed as a child and begin meeting those unmet needs from the past.

Anytime you experience a negative feeling state, you can take this as a plea for attention from your inner child. Close your eyes and ask your inner child what he or she is trying to tell you. Comfort the child and realize what that does for your feelings.

Repeat your inner child work at least two or three times a week. Each time you may see many different aspects of yourself. Comfort your inner child, and accept the pain and anger the child has not been allowed to express. As you do inner child work, you become your own parent. Create a kind, loving and compassionate parent for your inner child. Your unconscious accepts, as a part of your total reality, what you do. The purpose of reworking the past is to release it.

But don't stop there. Continue to work with your inner child, providing experiences you never had. Visualize your inner child at the zoo, at birthday parties, and help him or her with schoolwork. Be there for your child. Teach your inner child to trust in life. Help your inner child believe that life is self-affirming. In this way, you build a foundation based on confidence and security.

Chapter Fifteen

Eye Movement Therapy

Ellen's rape changed her life. Plagued by panic attacks and constant anxiety for twenty years, she suffered from Rape Trauma Syndrome, a form of Posttraumatic Stress Disorder. She had frequent, terrible nightmares. When she was alone, she was filled with dread. The rapist was never apprehended. Ellen feared he would come back and make good his promise to kill her. She felt terrified, victimized, powerless, and frozen.

The rape trauma had lodged in her nervous system, unable to be processed and integrated. It continued to spark so that any time she saw a man walking down the street, she felt victimized, powerless and worthless.

During a hypnosis session, Ellen visualized herself in a *safe place.* She instantly felt a lessening of the fear and anxiety. She supported the hypnosis by daily visualizations of personal safety, and repeated affirmations that she was safe and in control. By the next session, the anxiety had continued to lessen and her trust level in therapy had increased. She was now ready to move on to the Eye Movement Therapy.

Ellen's session went like this:

Jean: What is the image you have most often in your mind when you feel the fear?

Ellen: (She corrects me) I always feel the fear, Jean. I see him standing over me with the knife from my kitchen. His breath smells of alcohol. He says he's going to kill me in the morning, after he rapes me again.

Jean: Ellen, would you scan your body for signs of tension. Where do you feel the fear most in your body?

Ellen: Oh, that's easy. It's in my chest. I always feel that something heavy is lying on my chest. It even makes it hard for me to even get my breath. (She puts her hand over her heart area.)

Jean: What are you saying to yourself while this is going on.

Ellen: My life is over. He's going to kill me.

Jean: On a scale of 1 to 10, what would you say your anxiety level is at this moment.

Ellen: It's about a 7 now. It was usually a 10 before last week.

Jean: What I want you to do now is concentrate on the image in your mind, as well as your internal statements you just told me, along with what you're experiencing in your body. Do you think you can do that?

Ellen: Sure. I live with it every day.

Jean: Okay, now watch my two fingers as I move them back and forth across your field of vision. (Ellen moves her eyes, but has frequent glitches and loses track of my fingers. I start over and go a little slower.) Now, scan your body again, and rate your anxiety level and your belief statement that you are going to die.

Ellen: That was amazing. I already feel the heaviness lifting off my chest. You know what? That rape always seemed like it just happened. But now it seems like it's really in the past. I always thought people were good. But that man was really mean. I guess that there are just some mean people in the world.

Jean: You're right, Ellen. Not everyone has your best interests at heart. It helps to be selective to whom you give your trust. What does the image look like to you now?

Ellen: It's there. I know it happened. But I'm not afraid of it anymore. Somehow, it no longer seems as threatening.

Jean: How would you rate your current anxiety?

Ellen: It's about a 4. Some of it's still there, but I mostly feel relieved.

Jean: What about thinking you're going to die?

Ellen: That's gone. I did the best I could. I saved my life. You know, about midway through the eye movements, I remembered how much I used to like to paint. I think I'll start that again.

After doing the eye movements, Ellen felt the experience was actually in the past. She recognized she did the best she could at the time and that because of her quick thinking and actions, she had saved her life. She even remembered a hobby that she used to love, and soon started painting with oils. During the next several sessions, she brought several of her art works to therapy. She was, indeed, very talented.

Ellen made a full recovery within nine weeks, able to sleep peacefully and go out in public as she pleased, without anxiety. It was as if a new life had opened up for her. Ellen was a mentally healthy woman prior to her single incidence of rape trauma. That was part of the reason her symptoms remitted so quickly. Another aspect of her rapid recovery was due to the therapeutic use of the eye movements. This technique shortened her stay in therapy.

WHAT IS EYE MOVEMENT THERAPY

Eye Movement Therapy is a popular new technique that uses saccadic eye-movements to integrate and process trauma. It is used for phobias, fears and Posttraumatic Stress Disorder (nightmares, flashbacks, intrusive thoughts) caused by rape, childhood sexual abuse, and anxiety. It is frequently used for veterans with PTSD at many of the VA hospitals around the country.

It works best with healthy adults who have suffered a single trauma. Agoraphobia and other phobias have also responded simply and well. I have also used it with women who have eating disorders and have had success in helping them stop the obsession with their appearance and weight.

Eye Movement Therapy can also be used for other problems such as, self-esteem issues related to both upsetting past events and present life circumstances. It offers a method for defusing the force of negative memories that generate disturbing emotions and limiting beliefs about oneself and the world. Once defusing takes place, a dramatic shift in beliefs and spontaneous changes in behavior are often experienced.

Some of my clients now complain they have dropped old defense mechanisms so fast, thus overcoming years of suffering, that they have to go through a period of adjustment to become acclimated to their new ways of being.

With people for whom major and minor traumas have been woven into the very fabric of their personality and memory, Eye Movement Therapy is much slower, and should be used only as part of an overall treatment approach. It certainly can't do everything.

Many incest victims, because they felt so isolated and powerless when they were growing up, have missed out on life skills that other children naturally acquire. Once they are no longer preoccupied with their disturbing memories, they usually discover they do not know how to say "no," assert themselves at work, or be intimate in their relationships. These skills cannot be taught by doing eye movements alone; they require practice and the development of habits.

In cases where incest survivors whose traumas in childhood were repeated and often brutal, the eye movements can help, but gentleness and care must be taken about how much they can handle and integrate, and at what pace.

HOW DOES EYE MOVEMENT THERAPY WORK

There is no research about how Eye Movement Therapy actually works. The theory is that it works because it replicates the eye movements of REM sleep (dreaming), which causes the brain to finally process and solve a blocked trauma or problem that was somehow locked into the nervous system and never fully processed.

Traumatic experiences are not processed or integrated by the brain due to the overwhelming feelings of powerlessness that occur. They remain locked in the nervous system, much like a piece of shrapnel from a explosion imbedded deep in the skin. It festers, becomes irritated, and causes constant pain.

Eye Movement Therapy appears to access the information processing system, similar to the one found in REM (rapid eye movement) sleep. When the information processing system is triggered by the rapid eye movements, the disturbing memories are then processed and integrated rapidly. This removes much stress and pressure, even for traumatic experiences that happened early in life.

USES FOR EYE MOVEMENT THERAPY

Eye Movement Therapy is best used in conjunction with an overall plan of recovery. It is only one technique, among many, that may be used on the path to wholeness. It helps unblock early traumatic experiences and the resulting negative belief patterns.

Eye Movement Therapy allows people to rapidly work through their traumatic memories. It does not develop new coping and behavioral skills. These must be learned as the old self-destructive survival behaviors and beliefs are extinguished. The removal of these blockages then makes a space for new learning to take place.

A word of caution:
- This technique is not for everyone, and it is useful only under certain conditions. Not everyone benefits from it, but those who do, usually make substantial gains.
- Do not use this technique without a therapist if you are emotionally unstable, impulsive, or at risk for suicide.

- If you suspect you have some personality fragmentation, as most abuse victims do, then you should seek the assistance of a therapist trained in Eye Movement Desensitization and Reprocessing (EMDR). Otherwise, should you attempt this by yourself, you might trigger a personality fragment to arise spontaneously and/or dissociate, leaving you frightened and bewildered. A therapist can help you process and integrate what comes up.
- Do not do the eye movements if they make your eyes hurt.
- You must have a *safe place* firmly established within. Do the eye movements after you are securely in your *safe place*. Otherwise, you may retraumatize yourself.
- Stay in the present as you do the eye movements. Allow the material that comes up to flow through you without getting stuck in it.
- Be sure also to have a support network in place or a trusted friend to whom you can share and process your experiences.
- If you are unable to establish a *safe place*, or you are hesitant to try it after all these warnings, by all means seek the assistance of a therapist trained in Eye Movement Desensitization and Reprocessing (EMDR).
- Be sure you have established a firm bond of trust and feel safe and secure in your therapist's presence before you start the eye movements.
- Arrange for a predetermined signal such as a hand raise to say STOP if you become uncomfortable.

The reason for these precautions is that it is probable that you will trigger a reenactment of a traumatic memory. It won't last long and may be necessary for complete integration to take place. If you do not have the appropriate safe guards in place, you may retraumatize yourself, and that's not helpful.

When the traumatic memories are triggered, *DO NOT STOP* the eye movements if at all possible, until the processing is complete. However, if you feel it's too much for you, then stop and process what happened. While doing the eye exercises, remain anchored in the present time, and keep the memories flowing. The following is the protocol for Eye Movement Therapy. It is not etched in concrete, and you may vary it according to your needs once you understand the technique.

EYE MOVEMENT THERAPY TECHNIQUE

Hold the first three listed items in your mind while you do the eye movements.

1. Create a single image from the trauma you wish to deal with. This is usually the memory that is the focus of the disturbing flashbacks.
2. Recall what words you have thought about yourself or the incident that goes best with the image. This may take the form of a belief statement such as, "I'm powerless," "I'm out of control" or, "I did something wrong."
3. Scan your body up and down, noticing where you feel fear and tension. These feelings may be similar to the feelings and body sensations, such as fear and an overwhelming adrenaline rush, which occurred during the original trauma.
4. Rate the level of your anxiety and distress, on a scale of 1 to 10. 0 = no anxiety; 10 = the highest anxiety possible.
5. Rate your belief on a scale of 1 to 7; 1 = completely untrue, 7 = completely true.
6a. If you are with a therapist, the therapist's two fingers, or hand, is moved slowly back and forth across the field of your vision, horizontally, from the extreme left to the extreme

right, at a distance of 12 to 24 inches from your face. When tracking is established, the speed will be increased to, two back-and-forth movements, per second. This is repeated 24 times. These movements may be extended more times if there is difficulty processing the information.

6b. If you choose to do this by yourself, select two objects on which to focus, one at the extreme left and one at the extreme right of your field of vision. Move your eyes back and forth to look at them. Then selectively, move your eyes back and forth horizontally, in the same manner described above. If there are glitches in your eye movements, as there frequently are, guide your eyes back on track and continue the process until all the eye movements have been made.

6c. If you become dizzy or develop a headache when you first start, change directions. Use either vertical, circular or diagonally sweeps. If it doesn't get better, stop.

7. End the last eye movement in mid-sweep, and take a deep breath and say to yourself, "Let it go."

8. What are you noticing now? Talk these feelings and images out with your therapist, trusted friend or support network. Debriefing is very important.

9. Check your anxiety level, and rate it from 1 to 10. Compare it with your previous rating. It should be down.

10. Check your belief statement. Has it changed to a positive one?" "It wasn't my fault," is stated with a negative (not) in the sentence. A positive statement is, "I did the best I could."

11. Notice if there is a shift in your overall body toward relaxation. Rate your relaxation, images, anxiety and belief statements each time you do the eye movements.

12. Repeat the eye movements each time there is a shift, until the anxiety level in down to 0 or 1, and the negative belief statement has inwardly changed to a positive one.

Each time the eye movements are accomplished, the internal images may change. After each set of eye movements ask, "What do I get now." Listen for words that have no fear. That is because once you release the traumatic material, more may come to take it's place. It's like cleaning out a closet that's stuffed full of things which are no longer useful. Keep working at it until it's all gone. It may take 3 to 15 sets of eye movements for one session.

Scan your body for any remaining signs of tension. If you find other tension, as you probably will, it may be another unprocessed series of traumatic events. You certainly can't do it all in a day.

Give yourself plenty of time in between doing the eye movements so you can get used to the new changes. Write down any dreams you may have as they will probably reflect the changes going on internally.

You might also open up areas about which you may have not been aware. Previously blocked memories of conflict and turmoil from childhood may arise.

Unblocking a major defense is like breaking a dam. The water gushes through and washes out. You keep going upstream until all the dams are broken open. It's a lot like solving a riddle. You never really know where the end of it is, until you get there.

When I see glitches in eye movements as the client follows my hand sweeps with her eyes, I recognize it as a sign that something is going on internally. I slow down the eye movements to make it easier for her eyes to follow my hand and to process what's coming up. The comment I most often hear, after doing the eye movements is, "I am more relaxed."

A colleague in another city called to tell me of an incident involving a patient at a VA hospital where the eye movements had been used during a group therapy. The patient had become lost and disoriented while driving home along a familiar route.

This is an example of why it is wise to first see a therapist skilled in Eye Movement Desensitization and Reprocessing (EMDR). Obtain a clinical assessment as to your readiness to use this technique. Be certain and finish all the processing after the eye movements. This helps the integration process and also determines if you have loosened up something that needs further work.

The eye movements don't take away anything that's supposed to be there and they don't give a person amnesia. Eye movements make a presupposition that there is inherent goodness and worthiness in everyone. By removing the blockages, you can make giant leaps toward the wholeness of your real self.

Chapter Sixteen

The Healing Dream

Beverly reported a dream about a subject she had long been working on in therapy. While she was married to Bob, she began having panic attacks and flashbacks about her childhood sexual abuse. Bob and Beverly eventually divorced and her life vastly improved. However, she still had to deal with the sexual abuse.

Beverly's Dream

Beverly dreamed she was at a social gathering with her elderly grandfather who had molested her as a child. She didn't know everyone there. In the dream, a man comes over to her and indicates he thinks Beverly and her grandfather have a romantic attachment. He offers to introduce Beverly to a man more appropriate for her. Beverly replies that her companion is her *grandfather* and she doesn't understand how the man could think she was involved with her grandfather.

Then Beverly notices a table full of used merchandise. A pile of books and tapes on many different subjects are on the floor. Beverly thinks they belong to her grandfather.

The scene changes. She is still with her grandfather. They are looking at an oversized fireplace with two grates in it. Beverly's mother now comes into the picture, and she is moving bellows back and forth, fanning the flames in the fireplace. The mother, an accomplished musician, plays Requiem by Mozart. She does this by somehow attaching the bellows to one of the grates and continues to fan the flames.

At the end of the music, the mother lifts the grate high. This reminds Beverly of arching her back while in sexual orgasm. A burning log with limbs changes to look like a roast turkey. The dream ends.

Dream Interpretation

Beverly interpreted the dream by first saying that she hadn't recalled everything that had happened between herself and her grandfather. Prior to the dream, she had been aware of only one aspect of him (Dr. Jekyll).

During the ensuing session, Beverly recalled not only how the family had placated him, but also how he had "gaslighted" her grandmother (he would mouth words to his wife and then start talking out loud. He would then accuse her of going deaf.). The table of used merchandise had symbolized to Beverly that she had once felt as if she were used merchandise, a possession of her grandfather's. During the therapy session Beverly began to see the problem as belonging to her grandfather. By changing the symbolism to that of the grandfather being financially tight (would only purchase used merchandise), she no longer had to hold on to her former feeling of being used goods.

Beverly also saw that her grandfather was well versed on many different topics (the books and tapes on the floor), and that she had inherited some of his better qualities. Beverly also liked to study and learn new things.

Beverly's original sexual identity of being used merchandise on the table had been rated more important in stature than her artistic, creative and scholarly abilities. She knew they were lower in value because the books and tapes were placed on the floor. By seeing these things as the possessions of her grandfather, she had allowed him to define her sexual being and discount her talents.

During the therapy session, Beverly realized that her mother had used her for a sacrificial lamb (fans the flames) with the grandfather. She had made Beverly when a child sleep with him, even against Beverly's protests (her bellows).

The mother grades (the grates) Beverly on her performance. Beverly's mother graded her in many ways. One was sexual (used merchandise), another was academic. No one paid any attention to the academic. The second grate in the fireplace was empty, signifying that Beverly had already resolved her sexual abuse issues with her father.

In adulthood, Beverly felt guilty about her sexuality. She put most of her efforts into her studies, where she could make better grades (than in marriages), but she still felt worthless. The mother graded Beverly throughout her life. Letters Beverly wrote her mother were graded, and mistakes were marked in red ink and sent back to her.

Beverly arrived at the end of her dream interpretation by realizing her attraction to her grandfather stemmed from her fantasy that he was one of the very few people from her childhood who had been nice to her, albeit his niceness had been motivated through using her. Beverly didn't fail to recognize that she had been served up as a piece of meat (the turkey) to him.

The orgasm and roast turkey also signified to Beverly that she was "done with that part of her life." The orgasm was a "little death." Beverly "had risen" above her sexual abuse and the need for her mother's approval. The part of her that had died was reborn.

Beverly related the dream to an experience in her current life. The dream had occurred the night she and a man she was hopeful about establishing a relationship, gazed at a roaring fire in her fireplace.

After the dream, she realized the man was a lot like her grandfather. He was extremely intelligent, well versed, and even resembled her grandfather at a younger age. Beverly now suspected she needed to look deeper into the relationship before she became any more involved.

• • •

Dreams have long been known as the royal road to the unconscious. The author of the dream is the only person who knows the true meaning of the dream, according to the writings of Carl Jung.

Although some symbols are universal, the way they are interpreted is highly personal and depends on the dreamer's history and background. For example, animals often represent the instinctual aspect of the dreamer. But if one person was bitten in childhood by a dog, and another person's dog was their best friend, each will interpret the dog symbol differently in their dreams.

Children in a dream are usually rooted in childhood conflict and represent the dreamer's inner children, or different aspects of her personality. A baby can represent some new undertaking or a new part of the personality that is emerging. Likewise, people can die in the dream, sometimes violently. The death can represent that a part of them has died.

Dreams that indicate a lack of nurturing in early childhood are those with themes of negative images, such as deserted cities and natural catastrophes. They may contain critical dialogue, telling the dreamer she is worthless and/or undeserving of decent treatment. Abuse dreams can emerge as conflicts where the dreamer is overwhelmed and threatened with knives or guns or in a car with no brakes (out of control). For example, one abuse victim frequently dreamed that a bald-headed man was chasing her with a knife. Another client dreamed of a man chasing her with a baseball bat.

Dreams reveal the hopes and wishes of the dreamer. They also reveal the fears, anxieties, intuitions and the unacknowledged aspects of the self (known as the shadow side). Dreams can solve problems and teach new ways of coping with situations and people. But, most of all, dreams are a reflection of the divine. They can teach you about your inner self, give guidance, and heal what seems to be insurmountable wounds on all levels of your being—emotional, mental, physical and spiritual.

Dreams can give answers for your life and thereby reduce stress. Any question you have can be answered by your dreams. In order to enlist the help of dreams, it is important to remember them. In our culture, dreams are often ignored and dismissed as irrelevant. When you consciously place value on dreams, you are more likely to remember them. It may, however, take some practice and effort. Until you can remember your dreams, write down how you feel immediately after the dream.

Tips to help you remember your dreams:
- Learn to wake up without an alarm clock. Dreams are very fragile and evaporate like the morning mist if you jar awake.
- Upon awakening, stay in the dreaming position with your eyes closed. The body has cellular memory. Staying, or getting back into the sleeping position, may help you recall the dream.
- Write your dream down immediately upon waking up as you may not remember it later.
- Put forth a sincere effort to remember your dreams. Tell yourself before you go to sleep, "Upon awakening, I will remember a dream."
- Suggest to yourself that you will awaken during the night after a significant dream. When you do, write it down then.
- The "drink of water technique for creative problem solving through dreaming" also helps in remembering dreams. It consists of filling a glass full of water. Drink half of it before you go to bed as you think of a question or problem for which you want answers in the dream. Upon awakening, drink the other half of the water. Believe the answers are coming to you. Your answers may appear then, or hours, or days, later.
- The American Indians used dream catchers* placed over their beds to catch bad dreams in the web and held there until the burning sun's rays evaporated them with the dew. Good dreams simply slipped through the center hole in the web. These unique symbols are not only decorative, they emphasize the importance of dreams in your life.

*Handmade dream catchers are available from Deb Stone, (918) 749-2169

Recording Your Dreams

Dreams are important for your overall health and well being. Not everyone remembers dreaming, but we all dream about one and a half hours in eight hours of sleep. This calculates to an average of four to seven dreams per night. Dreaming is essential. Research on dream deprivation has proven that people who are dream deprived experience anxiety, irritability, and difficulties in concentration. Alcohol and drug usage decrease dreaming.

Once you are able to remember your dreams, even bits and pieces of them, it is important to write them down immediately as they are quickly forgotten. Another reason to record them immediately is so that you can later analyze the word you use to describe them. For example, the word "apparent" used in describing a dream could really mean "a parent."

Create a "dream journal" that you use for no other purpose than to write down your dreams. Use a pen with a small light attached to it that you use for no purpose other than recording your dreams. Keep it on the bedside table, while you sleep. If you have a dream during the middle of the night, record it then; don't wait until morning.

Draw a line through the middle of the page of your dream journal, dividing the page in half. On the top half, draw the dream, its symbols and emotions with colored pencils. On the bottom half, write down the dream in the present tense using verbs. For instance, "I see a house surrounded by tall and beautiful red and yellow flowers. Then I notice an upstairs open window where the curtains are blowing outside. The room is dark inside, but I hear someone calling me from there."

Record every detail you can remember. You may want to skip every other line, so when you go back to fill in later, the space will be there. Read the recorded dream over every day and review it in your mind while you continue to work on the dream.

More meanings may come to you. Circle words that mean more than one thing. Dreams are layered with multiple meanings. Each symbol or segment can stand alone, creating additional interpretations. You may find up to ten different interpretations for your dream, so leave plenty of space to record them.

After you have recorded your dream, give it a title. Then read it out loud. Sometimes the words give clues as to what the dream means. Ask yourself, "What is the dream trying to tell me?" "In what part of my waking life do I feel the same way I felt in the dream?"

In a separate notebook, mark each page with a letter from the alphabet "A" through "Z." In this notebook, alphabetically record the different symbols from your dreams and what they mean to you. For example, on the "A" page, you would draw the symbol apple, and then write down what that symbol means to you. On page "S" you would draw a snake, and then write what that symbol means to you. Keep the dream journal under your pillow when you are not sleeping.

Ten Entrances To The Dream
1. Begin with the most difficult and subtle question of all: what is the underlying emotional theme of the story? When viewed from a distance, what is the feel of the dream's prevailing emotion? What holds it together?
2. Recall your own recent, immediate experiences. Dreams are often sparked by the residue of yesterday's happenings.
3. Isolate and identify the primary elements of the dream text. What are the dreams components? One of the most common errors made in trying to understand a dream is the almost automatic refusal to recognize more than one character or element or verbal idea in the narrative when, of course, all the parts are indispensable.

4. Pay especially close attention to the seemingly trivial details and the little discrepancies.
5. Do not allow embarrassment to distract attention from elements that make you uncomfortable. Disgust and dread are feelings frequently used to conceal deeper layers of your psyche.
6. What first occurred to you on remembering the dream and reading the dream text may be the most important thing.
7. Assume full responsibility for the dream. You may try to hide from your dreams by thinking of yourself as a passive movie screen upon which dreams are shown. You may refuse to believe that they are your own creations which you, as the dreamer, have authored. If the dream has an evil side, then it is also a side of you.
8. The dream can condense opposites into one truth.
9. The many aspects of the self often separate into different people in the dream. Everything in the dream comes from you. Each character. Each scene. Each object. You chose them. Ask why you made the story this way and not that way. You could have made it another way, but chose to cast it in this one. You are all the parts of the dream, even the ones you don't like.
10. Describe your role in the dream and distinguish what type of dream you had. Look at the issues in the dream, the emotional data, what the historical connection is to your life. What resolution came about as part of the dream process?

Make your dreams an actual part of your life. After you have a dream, celebrate the dream by acting out all the players in the drama. Understand what each has to tell you and the attitude each presents. Honoring and expressing gratitude for your dreams helps you remember them better. Give them the credit they deserve. Dreams are a wonderful, helpful, part of you.

Another important element in remembering dreams includes preparing your dream environment. Fill your bedroom with symbols of love, strength, and courage, and pictures that give you a sense of nurturing and safety. White walls and surroundings helps bring clarity to dreams.

If you are in therapy, obtain a picture of your therapist to put on your bedside table. This will help take the higher energy of the therapist into your dreams. A picture of Carl Jung, the noted dream analyst, would also be a good energy to bring in as well. Gazing at the eyes of a master teacher can create what hypnotists call, "deep trance identification."

When you are at "oneness" with the teacher, you may share the teacher's wealth of knowledge. Even though a master teacher such as Carl Jung is deceased, his spirit, strength, and knowledge are still available for you to draw on. The teacher's energy can improve the intensity, coloring, depth and archetypal quality of your dreams and promote healing, resolution, and understanding.

The symbols and pictures you place around you as you sleep influence your dreams. A messy bedroom, or watching a violent TV show in bed before going to sleep may also be reflected in a dream.

Keep your dream environment clean, surrounded with images of joy, and your thoughts positive while you drift off to sleep, as you take your total environment into your dreams.

Approach the dream as a mystery. Take the clues, the feelings, and the words, and weave then together to create your own meaning from the dream.

Read over the following types of dreams and identify as many types as you can remember having. The same dream may have more than one classification.

TYPES OF DREAMS

- *Amplifying:* Life situations or attitudes are heightened and brought to the dreamers attention.
- *Archetypal:* When you know which of the seven archetypes are energized, you have a better chance of dealing with the issue at a conscious level. For information on archetypal representations in dreams, please refer to *Understanding Dreams* by Mary Ann Matton or *Dreams and Healing* by John Sanford. Both Matton and Sanford are Jungian dream analysts.
- *Childhood:* Brings up old conflicts needing resolution. When you continue having childhood dreams, notice the mythic pattern that is reenacted over and over.
- *Compensatory:* A dream that presents a viewpoint about an issue which is different or contrary to your waking view point. The unconscious always knows where the center of balance is. This type of dream results in self-regulation and points ahead for solutions.
- *Confirming/Complementary:* The dream confirms an effective or meaningful choice you have made in your waking life.
- *Ego Issue:* You need to change some attitude, feelings and/ or behavior. This type of dream is trying to make this clear to you.
- *Expressive:* The imagery and feeling in this type of dream is almost impossible to express in your waking life—either by action or explanation.
- *Great:* A dream which contains a resolution of a major issue in your life—and new insight so deep that you feel the message.
- *Incubative:* When you go to sleep, you ask a question of

your dream. It can be a simple question about a lost article or a deep question abut the meaning of your life. In the morning you have an initial clue to the meaning of the dream because of the question you have asked.

- *Intuitive:* This dream gives you information about people or situations. It prepares you for some sort of action or resolution in your conscious waking life.
- *Issues:* Problems are presented to you so that you may take them further in your dream-work and resolve them.
- *Lucid:* You know that you are dreaming. You are in the dream and at the same time observing the dream. Your waking ego and dream ego are merged, producing an unusual conscious recognition that you are dreaming.
- *Nightmare:* Nightmares (in adults) are an urgent message from your unconscious about sometime that needs attention from you. If you have a nightmare, try to go back to sleep and make up another ending for it. A change of attitude before going to sleep may help you sleep through the dream.

Ancient cultures such as the Egyptians, Babylonians, Greeks, and Romans, all believed dreams to be an important source for the soul to receive guidance from the spiritual world. Throughout the Bible, numerous references are made about dreams. From the ancients to the present, people have learned how to influence their dreams through the thoughts and images they have just before falling asleep. This process is known as *dream incubation.* My own variation of it goes like this:

Before going to sleep at night, say a prayer and ask for help from your angels. Mentally visualize surrounding yourself in white light. Healing comes easier and faster using spiritual guidance. Your angels will do eighty percent of the work for you. When you are finished with your prayer, ask yourself to have a dream to show you guidance and to give you healing, or to dream about a certain topic. Gently affirm your willingness to remember your dreams.

Carefully select some symbolic objects that reflect the underlying mood and focus of the dream you wish to evoke. Carl Jung suggested repeating to yourself the topic of your prospective dream in a single sentence, such as, "I want the angels to open me to the love I did not receive in childhood so that I may accept my worthiness."

If you want to dream about a specific subject, or do problem solving in your dreams, you might even bring some suitable objects or mementos about the subject, into the bed with you, and sleep with them.

Write the phrase or single sentence in your dream journal, and calmly remind yourself to remember the dream upon awakening. Do not put any psychological pressure on yourself. Refuse to take any drugs or alcohol, because they suppress dreaming. However, a piece of rich chocolate before bedtime sometimes enriches the dream experience.

For each particular healing dream you wish to evoke, use this technique three days in a row, and continue making suggestions of healing and wholeness. Pleasant dreams.

VICTIM NO MORE

Chapter Seventeen

Empowerment For Survivors

Jana smiled softly. Her black hair had grown long and was pulled back in a pony tail, clearly showing the features of her face. Earlier in her therapy, her hair often partially covered her face as she had looked down at the floor when she talked. But now she no longer felt powerless.

"It's so sad that I used to think I had to hide a part of myself," she said. "Last week, I started to have a panic attack. I felt trapped staying in my friend's house, but my apartment was no longer safe. Robbers had broken in the door. Then I just went inside myself. It was all there; all the inner peace and tranquility I could have ever hoped for. The panic attack just went away. I'm so happy and grateful for all the wonderful things I have in my life."

Jana recounted how her life had changed over the past year. She had left Seattle and the drug scene there. She had learned to establish boundaries between herself and her mother. She had learned she could not only support herself financially, but she had a recent promotion in a job that she loved. All that, and a blossoming romance.

"I can't wait to introduce him to my father," she laughed. "Finally I feel I have a normal life. I just love the way things have turned out between my father and me. We've bonded—I love talking to him and telling him what's going on in my life. He understands without judging me."

"Jana," I said, "you've made a lot of changes. These things didn't happened all by themselves. Both you and your father have made an effort to get to know each other. Your consistent work with yourself made all the changes possible."

"I know. Do you realize I was only two years old when my parents divorced? I never had the chance to get to know him when I was living with my mother. I can't believe I used to think my step-mother was so mean. She's very nice, and I feel really close to her, too. It's hard to realize my life has turned around and that all these good things have opened up for me. I located a better apartment in a safer neighborhood. It's about the same price as the old one and it has a place for my art studio, too."

"Jana, you have found your inner power. You deserve all the good things that are coming your way. "

. . .

Accepting your own inner power is what empowerment is all about. Once you tap into your spiritual strength, you realize that you possess the ability to turn fear into compassion. You stop judging yourself and others. You accept yourself, and you accept others, just as they are. You accept that injustice occurs, with all the hurt, pain and anger that result from it. Even though you may have been hurt and betrayed, you are always worthy.

As you accept your worthiness at the deepest levels, you accept yourself on the level of the soul. You realize that true authentic power is internal, not external.

Power is something with which we all have to come to terms. The denial of this basic responsibility is to grant permission for others to extend their web of power over us. There are no permanent vacuums in life—any void is soon filled. If you don't own your power—someone else will take it. When anyone succeeds in obtaining power over you, it becomes domination. And that usually occurs because you give another the right to intimidate you.

Our culture is based on external power. Even the fashion myths foster beliefs that if you look just right, you can have what you want in life. That is simply not true. Addictions are also based on power as external. Whenever you swallow pills, buy something, diet, or engage in compulsive behavior to fill an inner emptiness, an illusion is created. At the same time that you are engaging in addictions in order to feel whole and powerful, you are being inwardly corrupted and spiritually depleted.

A belief in external power takes you far away from the truth of your real self. Your eyes then see through the eyes of the ego, the self-limiting perception of the personality that thinks it is all there is.

When you are overwhelmed by violence, there is a strong tendency to identify with the aggressor. You may see power as *power over*, not the *power to be*. At the heart of all violence is external power, the power to make someone else comply with the demands of another.

The aftermath of abuse often leaves you devoid of knowledge of an inner reservoir of power. When you are traumatized and fearful, you may think that's all there is to you because the fear seems so overwhelming. There is more to you than you are aware.

When you look back at your past, you may only see your childhood, your parents, and your particular situation. You may mistakenly think you are only a product of your environment and previous experiences. But there is more, much more, than you can consciously comprehend.

True power is personal power. It comes from within. You are the director in the drama of your life. Personal power allows you to be what you are as a result of your own intentions, instead of the misguided actions of others.

Personal power implies you accept the responsibility for your own life. It means controlling your abilities to draw upon and focus on your inner resources. It allows you to work with your own actions and goals toward meaningful pursuits.

Personal power means:
- Your posture is straight and erect. It conveys confidence.
- Your ego may be put to the side when relating to others.
- You are able to maintain your own point of view while others are allowed to express their opinions.
- You use "I" statements and make eye contact.
- You don't paint yourself into a corner by making demands on others.

- You can change your mind in the light of new information.
- You don't insist others agree with you.
- You don't go to the opposite extreme when others demand agreement from you.
- You do what is in your own best interest.
- You choose your own time and place for confrontation.
- You have a spiritual belief to sustain you when problems arise.

Personal power gives you the power to tell the story of what happened to you. It also gives you the power to grieve the life and security you lost. And, best of all, it provides the power to conceptualize and build a new and stronger life.

There is a place in each of us, beyond the fear, beyond the anger, that is divine. It is your right to claim your own birthright—your divinity. Look beyond your biological parents and your woundings to the wisdom of your soul.

Mourning and grieving your losses is necessary for healing. New research reports that the basis of Posttraumatic Stress Disorder is delayed and unresolved grief.

Crying and grieving helps the distressed brain chemistry to normalize. Without doing the grief work, nothing may change. Many survivors fear that if they ever let down and start grieving, they will never stop. They fear they will be consumed by their tears.

As the fear of grieving approaches their awareness, many survivors dream of drowning in a dark and turbulent sea—the sea of their tears. It takes the light of your inner strength to face this darkness. But like the sunshine after a storm, the tears do end. A new day, and a new life, unfolds.

True healing involves making a connection with the spiritual part of yourself. You are never truly whole and complete without the acceptance of it. The spiritual part of yourself is always there, even if you are not consciously aware of it. It is a part of you. You cannot lose it. The divine within knows the truth and what is best for you, even when you do not.

Your divine being can reveal unknown truths to you. Keep what you want to know in the forefront of your mind. Repeat the following phrase frequently for several days in a row: "The truth has within itself the power to reveal itself." Pay attention to signs that appear to you. They may contain the answers you've been waiting for.

You may not trust your own perceptions, feelings or intuitions. You've been taught to deny reality. Defenses, such as denying your feelings, once helped you survive in an abusive home environment. When old defenses, like denial, have become so much a part of you, letting them go can cause apprehension—you may fear nothing will be left.

Finding your own truth is essential to your recovery. When you disallow your sensory perceptions, you create enormous blockages between yourself and your divine being. This can be overcome. Learning to trust yourself, your intuitions, and your feelings, helps open the way to the spiritual connection.

The first step is to trust in the wisdom of your own soul to guide and lead you. The direction may be unfamiliar. Pay attention to, and trust, your instincts, feelings, intuitions, dreams and perceptions. Learn the differences between them so that you will know the source of your information.

Feelings come from thoughts that come from beliefs. Beliefs come from learned information that is based on past experiences, your parents and our culture. You can change unhealthy beliefs to healthy ones and, therefore, change the way you feel about things. Perceptions are your interpretation of your feelings about things, people, events and situations.

Instincts come from your animal nature and are concerned mainly with survival. However, if an abusive past situation is not completely processed, it is possible to identify a situation as dangerous when it actually is not.

Intuitions come from your Higher Power, and as such may be revealed through a thought that darts through your mind, a quiet knowing, or an inner voice. Intuitions are usually right. Unlike instincts, intuitions lack the urgency of feelings. You can choose or not choose to believe in, or act on, intuitions.

All of your senses affect you. Allow them to teach and lead you to your own truth. I've heard so many clients say, "Why didn't I do such and such. I knew, I just knew it. But I didn't pay attention to myself." It takes courage to trust and believe in yourself.

Ask the Divine to heal and comfort you and give you strength and courage; courage to face the pain, and the strength to go beyond it. In so doing, you will reach into deeper and deeper areas of the self. Eventually the changes come.

When all your parts unite and come to know themselves, what was once a pile of personality fragments that seemed like charcoal briquets, can become a beautiful, many sided, faceted, diamond. Your Divine Being can be a constant inner source of inspiration, strength and courage in this endeavor.

Perhaps you have been on guard against danger. Combined with an inner struggle to hold yourself together, you may be unaware of some of your talents and abilities. When you make the spiritual connection, you enter into a larger dimension of yourself. You think about yourself differently.

• • •

To accept your Inner Self, your Divine Being, is enormously powerful. To accept divinity means that, in part, you have the same quality of life force as God. You have that same dimension available to you. You can draw upon it and work with it. It also means that in order for it to grow, develop, and expand, there needs to be an understanding of the power in your life. You need to understand how divine power functions.

Divine power offers you many choices and opportunities. A victim has no choices. A victim feels trapped. As a child, you were dependent on those around you to protect you. Sometimes they did. Sometimes they didn't. Sometimes you were abused. A victim's well-being, or lack of it, comes from the security she receives from her environment. A victim looks outside herself for the definition of herself. She looks for clues as to what feelings are appropriate. She is other directed.

When you accept your divine being, you learn to look within yourself for power, for comfort, and for security. You become inner directed. You decide for yourself what is in your best interest. You trust your inner being, and in so doing, you make the spiritual connection, and tap into that power.

Spiritual power, however, needs to be controlled and directed. When I was in college, I knew a graduate student who had been abused as a child. She was quite shy and timid when school started. However, after some therapy sessions, she became very vocal. She talked in every class and gave her opinions. In fact, she didn't leave much time for anyone else to talk. When you find out something new about yourself, you need to learn how to use it. Practice it. Get the experience of it. But learn how to control it. Just because you realize you have this power doesn't automatically give you good judgement about how to use it. For example, feel free to offer your opinions to others, but don't try to force your beliefs on them. Respect the rights of others to draw their own conclusions about what is best for them, even when you think you know better.

PRAYER

Connecting with the spiritual dimension is done in many ways. One of the ways that the ancients have recommended is prayer. Prayer is one of the most powerful ways you have of acknowledging the divine connection. Prayer itself is also one of the simplest ways of connection. In fact, many people feel that it can't work because it's too simple.

In prayer, you talk to God. You tell the Divine all about yourself just as you would a trusted friend. Don't hold back. Surrender to God all your insecurities, fears, anxieties, anger, depression, disappointments, hopes and your wishes.

You build a relationship with the Divine just as you would any other relationship by sharing your whole self. The connection cannot grow if you share only a mask or small portion of yourself. God accepts all of you, the good, bad and indifferent. From this unconditional acceptance, your experience of love and trust grows. Love is the opposite of fear. Love helps you release some of the negativity and fear that abuse causes.

Prayer is a state in which you place yourself in a receptive mode and stop pushing ideas and talk outward. You create an atmosphere of listening to an inner dimension of your being.

For centuries, people conceptualized God as something unobtainable for the ordinary person. God was thought of as some mysterious phantom-person floating around in the sky in a long white robe. But you can communicate with God. As you go inward through prayer to the source of life, you have an experience of the spiritual within yourself. The acceptance of your spiritual connection is enormously comforting. You learn to trust that there is an added dimension to yourself, something larger than your small, personal world.

Pray to the Divine with confidence and with a feeling of

closeness, as if you were a small child. A half-believing prayer is insufficient. Because of their disbelief, most people don't get any response. But if you talk to God with all your heart and make up your mind, "God will talk to me," and refuse to believe differently, one day it will happen.

Look for answers in dreams or things that stand out to you. An intuition that comes out of nowhere, something a child says, or words in a sign that strike your attention along the road, may be messages from God.

MEDITATION

Meditation can help you become aware of your spiritual connection to the source of life. In meditation, you go further into the stillness and quiet to attune your human consciousness with God's will. This creates a partnership and a strength you can draw on in all areas of your life.

The goal of meditation, much like prayer, is to make a spiritual connection with the source of your being. Meditation calms the mind, and dissolves negative attitudes, thoughts, and feelings. It takes off pressure, removes stress, and takes away the tendency to get caught, or trapped, in self created limitations.

Meditation allows you to see yourself—and how you created your own world from your illusions, perceptions, beliefs, fears, and habits. Until you are consciously aware of your motives and actions, you may live in disharmony with life. In meditation, you can view with understanding, your creation of the world.

In meditation, images that spring up are considered happenings of the mind. When you see them, or feel, or hear them, there is usually an experience of knowing and understanding what they are about. Do not allow yourself to become distracted by the images. That is not the concern of the meditator. The seeker in meditation seeks the spiritual. When images arise, they are simply observed and released. There is no need to remember or analyze them, because in meditation the light heals when you *let go*.

The discipline of meditation strengthens the ego and personality structure. By learning to *let go* of images, feelings, and thoughts that arise during meditation, you learn to discipline the mind. This carries over into all areas of your life. Then when fearful thoughts arise, you can say to yourself, *let go*, and return your mind to the task at hand. Meditation helps the structure of the personality reorganize in a more healthful and positive manner.

If you have a garden, you need to cultivate it and pull the weeds so what you grow has greater health and abundance. Think of your mind as a garden that needs tending. Meditation helps you become more aware of the thoughts you think, giving you greater power and control over them.

SPIRITUALITY AND THE ARTS

Divine experiences happen to people when they reach supreme ecstasy or great inspiration. If you've ever been to a concert and been in tune with the performers music, voice, or the instruments that they play, a part of you connects with a part of that person. There is a perception of something larger than yourself. If you've ever been to the theatre and experienced a connection with the actors and the drama, you will perceive the same invisible phenomenon. The connection is a larger vision of yourself and others. The degree of openness that you have given yourself to honor the divine dimension determines the depth of the experience.

The same is true for all the fine arts. When looking at a painting it is possible to connect with not only the artist but with the philosophy and spirituality of a society. Artists and craftsmen, when making art, are connecting with a basic inner self—a spiritual dimension. Cherish these experiences. They are about the spiritual connection.

THERAPY

Therapy also helps connect people to their inner self. Most individuals come for help only after they have failed in dealing with their problems and have exhausted all other possible resources. The reason self-healing is difficult is that it is not possible to heal on the same emotional and mental level that was present when the pain occurred. You grow through the pain and mature out of it.

Healing to wholeness is a four-fold process on the road to the spiritual connection. First comes the releasing, cleansing and clearing of the pain, hurt, anger, and negative issues. Second, comes the releasing of self-limiting beliefs, and replacing them with global, positive ones. The third step in the process involves the deepening of the self into the spiritual connection. The fourth, and final, leap is the acceptance of the spiritual connection and its guidance.

When you are wounded by betrayal and/or abuse, you learn not to trust others. You use whatever conscious will power you have in order to survive in a hostile environment. You may think you have to solve all your problems by yourself.

Accepting a spiritual connection involves turning your will power over to your Higher Power. By allowing your guidance to come from that source, you acknowledge your limitations as a mortal being. You don't have all the answers. You aren't perfect, and never can be. It is an enormous shift in perception and a leap of faith. The irony is that once you give up the struggle you are in better control of your life. Carl Jung, the famous Swiss psychiatrist, wrote extensively about the results of patients, that he saw over many years, in which he discovered tremendous connections to their own Higher Power.

TOOLS FOR SPIRITUAL GROWTH

One tool to help you see yourself in a more objective light is to imagine you are a writer. Visualize sitting in a comfortable chair, or at a table, looking out the window, at someone you love—your other self. Allow you, the writer, to be as open as possible. Write down whatever you know about that person you love. Her personality, struggles, fears, relationships, hopes and wishes.

Write down, as clearly as possible, all of her goals or premises. If she has too many directions, the act of writing them will help to clarify what she really seeks to accomplish and where her energies are fractured or scattered. If there aren't any goals or directions on the surface, the act of writing will help to focus upon areas that may need implementation, clarification, and resolution.

Realize that the content of your writing will take certain forms. Patterns will emerge; and from these patterns, you can see what her life and your life is about. Once you have become clear about the issues in your life—the ones you choose to deal with and those which are to be released—the act of emotional cleansing begins.

Releasing old worn-out images, attitudes, feelings and ways of being, can be achieved through visualizations, affirmations, prayer and meditation. They reinforce the desired way you choose to think and feel. Visualizations, affirmations, prayer and meditation all use spiritual energy, because they require a leap of faith. You put out something unto the unknown, with the faith that it will materialize.

Visualizations for healing

One visualization that assists in emotional and/or physical cleansing is to visualize yourself as Light. Project your body, as Light onto a mental view screen while in a relaxed state of mind. Image your problems as dark spots. Then imagine you have a ray gun and blast the dark areas with the Light from the ray gun. This technique is also very useful for physical problems such as breast tumors. Many women who stuff their feelings use their breasts as a dumping ground for their unacceptable feelings of anger, pain and resentment. You may strengthen the visualization by pointing a finger that is touching a tumor and image the Light shooting through your finger, destroying the tumor.

If the problem is connected to another person, then visualize the energy as a cord of color that connects the two of you. If it is a dark, amber, or red color, mentally burn a bright, white, light along the connecting cord from you to the other person. This will break the energy of negativity to that person.

The Light carries a positive charge. The darkness (hurt, anger, sadness, and grief) carries a negative charge and can drain you. Have you ever noticed how tired you get when you are depressed?

This is not to say that negative emotions are "bad." But, they need to be worked through and released. *You* are not your feelings. Feelings simply reflect where you are in thought and mood at any particular time.

Color visualizations are especially effective for releasing negative emotions and feelings. Breathing out the color red, for example, releases anger. Or, if you prefer, imagine you are blowing up red balloons and letting them float away from you. Be wildly creative in your visualization process. If you want to release a relationship, picture that person in a pink bubble and let it float away from you.

With an especially delicate relationship, first imagine walking in the direction of that person. Only go as close as you feel comfortable. Later, imagine that person before you. Talk to him and tell him everything you want to share with him. When you are finished, take his hands in yours, and embrace that person. Do not rush this. Allow yourself all the time you need. If possible, hold the embrace until you feel his pulse beat the same as your own. Continue to do this as long as you can. Repeat this visualization until you can do it without any negative feelings. When this is accomplished, that person has been released.

If you feel blocked in some area of your life, picture yourself driving a Jeep in your brain until you find the blockage. Then break it up with hammers and mentally haul it away. One client did this visualization and came upon the Great Wall of China. She used jack hammers and explosives to finally bring it down.

Each time you release an old feeling or image, give thanks for having had it, tell it you realize what it was doing for you, bless it and allow it to fade away. The act of blessing brings your energy forward from an inner place of love rather than from a place of fear. Fear holds the undesired idea or image, act, things or experience to you. Love helps you release.

Affirmations for healing

The power of affirmations can help bring the feelings, experiences, and conditions that you desire to your life. The purpose of an affirmation is to imprint the subconscious mind with new positive images and emotions. Write the affirmation using positive statements of success in the present tense and time on a 3 x 5 card. Carry it with you everywhere. Use the affirmation as often as necessary until it becomes a reality.

1. Read the affirmation out loud. (affirm it)
2. Vividly picture the end result.
3. Feel the emotion that will go with the accomplishment of your affirmation. Imagination x vividness = reality.

In quiet moments, say to yourself what you want, as though it has already happened. For example say, "I am healed now." "Release my fears and through me release ___ (the name of the person in the abusive relationship with you) fears. Fill my needs and through me fill ___ needs and let us experience a total belief in self." You would not, for example, say, I don't want _____." In this case, the unconscious does not hear the negative not, and may materialize what it is you don't want. Constant repetition will imprint the new reality. Mindless repetition will only create more doubt in your mind. Sincerity is very important. The true spirit behind the words will determine the outcome.

The spiritual power of affirmations and visualizations can draw situations to you. The power is greatest when your mind is clear. When energy is tied up in images of past attachments, hurts, wounds, pain or anger, you may not be as effective or clear in what you want at the present time.

When a clear spiritual connection is made, you have a sense of the larger self. You respond and are open to that power in your life. Now you may automatically assume as soon as that power comes into your life you are changed; you are different. That's true. But what you may fail to take into account is that even though you are changed as a result of that power becoming evident in your life, you still need to handle it. You've still got to learn how to deal with it, how to encompass it, how to use it and how to incorporate it into your life.

Take the experience of falling in love. That doesn't automatically give you good sense. Gross errors in judgement are often made when people are romantically inclined toward one another. Any new experience that is brought into your life is best taken by degrees into your life. Some people say, "But if you are really changed, then all the old passes away." This usually does not happen all at once.

The spiritual connection is enhanced as a result of your honest and deep inner desire to link with the source. But it doesn't happen out of belief. It happens out of action—what you are willing to commit yourself to do.

The spiritual connection cannot develop and expand unless you support those experiences in your life that allow the spiritual dimension to be honored. When you feel the prompting from the inner levels of the self that constantly call you to a deeper vision, to a larger perspective, to a more powerful outreach of the spirit, then that is the prompting that calls to you and says, "This is what you need to pursue in your life." That call is different for everyone, but it will give you guidance along your road to wholeness and connectedness.

Become an astute observer of life. Learn from what has happened in your own life. Become reflective about it, meditative about it, prayerful about it. Do not discount the experiences of your life that have been hurtful or painful. Do not discount the experiences of your life that have taken you into many different areas of human experience. All have their value. Some may be more difficult than others. Some may be more problematical than others and some may be more painful than others. But all have their value.

Allow yourself to see the place that all of them have taken. And the only way you can do that is to allow yourself to have some time to reflect on them. The time you spend in a meditative state, a prayful state, or a reflective mood, is very important to you.

The time you spend with men and women who have a commitment in their own lives to something larger than themselves is time well spent. Pay attention to the people you surround yourself with so that you can always allow your own being to become larger and fuller and deeper. You will not grow, or deepen, if your commitment is to limitation. You will not honor the spiritual connection if you commitment is to playing the *victim role*.

If you allow the spiritual dimension of yourself to open, if your commitment is to heal and go beyond your woundings—to the excellence of your being—you will move forward. Acceptance of the injustice done to the self is the beginning of empowerment. It takes as much courage to take a step away from the trauma as it does to encounter it. It's like saying, "It's all over. I did the best I could. It's time to go on."

Your suffering does have meaning. It can awaken you to the inner-most depths of your being. The deeper the wound, the deeper you go into the Light in order to heal. When you are made to feel powerless due to overwhelming assault, you know that your own personal will and concept of external power is insufficient to restore you to balance. Reach beyond yourself to your larger dimension—your spiritual power.

Appendix

DANGER ASSESSMENT*

Using a calendar, please mark the approximate dates during the past year when you were beaten by your husband or partner. Look for patterns. Write down if you started an argument, "just to get it over with." Write on that date in approximate hours how long each incident lasted and rate the incident according to the following scale:

1. Slapping, pushing; no injuries and/or no lasting pain
2. Punching, kicking; bruises, cuts, and/or continuing pain
3. Beat up; severe contusions, burns, broken bones
4. Threat to use weapon; head injury, internal injury, permanent injury
5. Use of weapon; wounds from weapon

Read over the following questions and put a check mark by each question which you answer yes.

1. Has the physical violence increased in frequency over the past year?
2. Has the physical violence increased in severity over the past year?
3. Has a weapon, or threat with weapon, been used?
4. Has he ever tried to choke you?

5. Is there a gun in the house?
6. Has he ever forced you into sex against your wishes?
7. Does he use drugs; amphetamines, speed, angel dust, cocaine, "crack," street drugs, heroin, or mixtures?
8. Does he threaten to kill you and/or do you believe he is capable of killing you?
9. Is he drunk every day or almost every day?
10. Does he control most or all of your daily activities?
11. Have you ever been beaten by him while you were pregnant?
12. Is he violently and constantly jealous of you? (Does he say "If I can't have you, no one can?")
13. Have you ever threatened or tried to commit suicide?
14. Has he ever threatened or attempted suicide?
15. Is he violent toward your children?
16. Is he violent outside of the home?

Add up the check marks. The higher the number of checks you have the more severe danger you are in.

*Used by permission of the Family Violence and Sexual Assault Institute, Tyler, Texas

INJURIES TO WOMEN FROM DOMESTIC VIOLENCE

- One woman in three will be assaulted during her lifetime by a domestic partner. (AMA, 1992)
- A woman is abused every twelve to fifteen seconds.
- About one thousand five hundred women are killed by their mates each year. That calculates to one woman every six hours.
- Four million women are beaten each year by their husband or boyfriend. (AMA, 1992)
- Domestic violence is the leading cause of injury to women (2,100,000 injuries annually), causing more injuries than muggings, stranger rapes, and car accidents, combined.
- Every year, domestic violence causes almost one hundred thousand days of hospitalization, thirty thousand emergency room visits, and forty thousand trips to the doctor.
- Fifty percent of all female emergency room admissions (not just trauma victims) are battered women.
- Women make 1,453,437 medical visits per year for treatment of injuries resulting from assault by a spouse.
- At least twenty-five percent of the women who are victims of domestic violence in the U.S. are beaten while pregnant. Two hundred forty thousand pregnant women in the U.S. are battered each year by their spouses or partners, or about six percent of all pregnant women. (CDC Report 3/94)
- Forty percent of all on-the-job deaths of women are homicides, many killed by their domestic partners.
- More than three million children witness acts of domestic violence every year.
- More than half of the men who abuse their wives also abuse their children. More than half of abused women who are mothers also beat their children.

- Children of abused mothers are six times more likely to attempt suicide and fifty percent more likely to abuse drugs and alcohol.
- In a thirty-six month study of one hundred forty-six children ages eleven to seventeen, from homes where wife-beating was a major problem, all the sons over the age of fourteen attempted to protect their mothers and sixty two percent of them were injured in the process.
- Every month, more than fifty thousand U.S. women seek restraining or protective orders.
- Fifty percent of all homeless women and children are fleeing domestic violence.
- Half of the victims of rape reported to police in 1992 were girls younger than eighteen. About one in six was under twelve. Most of the girls were raped by relatives or friends. (Justice Department, 1994)
- There are over one thousand shelters for battered women in the U.S., yet for every woman given shelter, many more are turned away.
- Of the thirty five women on death row in 1993, almost half were there for the murder of an abusive partner.
- An estimated seventeen percent of domestic violence complaints to police are made by men.
- The majority of abusive men do not voluntarily go to batterers' programs.
- If all female victims of domestic violence in 1993 joined hands, the line would stretch from New York City to Los Angeles.

Appendix

SAMPLE LETTER TO A SEXUAL HARASSER

Date

Dear (Harasser's name)

I am writing this letter to inform you that I do not welcome and feel (uncomfortable) (intimidated) (threatened) (angered) by your action (s). The action (s) I am referring to (include):

Examples:
On or around January 24, 1995, you left a magazine on my desk that I consider obscene. When I asked if it was yours, you claimed that you thought that I would be interested in the subject.

On three separate occasions, starting on the second day of my employment, you followed me into the supply closet to hug me and fondle my breasts.

You booked only one hotel room for the two of us at the engineering association conference in Phoenix and changed the reservation only after I insisted in front of the clerk that I have a separate room. At the banquet that evening you told me that I was "jeopardizing our working relationship and my position" with my "unfriendliness."

This behavior is offensive to me and constitutes sexual harassment. This (these) incident(s) has (have) created a (unprofessional) (tense) (stressful) working environment that interferes with my job performance, particularly in any matters that require contact with you. Therefore, I am asking you to stop this illegal harassment now.

Sincerely,

PERSONALITY FRAGMENTATION CHECK LIST

Read over the following list and mark the ones that apply to you. If you mark over three, seek a therapist skilled at treating personality fragmentation.

___ 1. The presence of amnesia, loss of time, or time distortion.
___ 2. Failure to improve in psychotherapy or by drug management.
___ 3. Three or more prior diagnoses with rapid fluctuations in symptoms or confusing or contradictory symptoms.
___ 4. Has both body ailments and psychiatric symptoms.
___ 5. Severe headaches, usually refractory to treatment (indicative of competition between personalities for control of the body, resulting in simultaneous and contradictory cortical signals sent through the cranial nerves).
___ 6. Hearing of voices within the head (80%) perceived as coming from within the head rather than from external sources (most auditory hallucinations of schizophrenics are experienced as external).
___ 7. Reports by others of uncharacteristic behavior that the person cannot recall.
___ 8. Discovery of unfamiliar objects, clothing, or writings in your possession that you cannot account for or recognize, or reports of being called by an unfamiliar name or of being known by others that you don't know.
___ 9. The use of "we" when you talk about yourself.
__10. A history of childhood trauma or abuse, usually accompanied by large memory gaps of childhood.
__11. The elicitation of alternate personalities through hypnosis or through spontaneous switching.
__12. Depression is a constant symptom.

Bibliography

Aburnene, Patricia; and Naisbitt, John. *Megatrends For Women*, Fawcett Columbine, New York, N.Y., 1992.

Achterberg, Jeanne. *Woman As Healer*, Shambhala, Boston, MA., 1991.

Allen, Charlotte Vale. *Daddy's Girl*, Berkley, New York, N.Y., 1980.

Armstrong, Louise. *Kiss Daddy Goodnight*, Pocket Books, New York, N.Y. 1978, 1987.

Asher, Alexis. *Please Don't Let Him Hurt Me Anymore*, Burning Gate Press, Los Angeles, CA., 1994.

Asper, Katherine. *The Inner Child In Dreams*, Shambhala, Boston, MA., 1992.

Barnett, Ola; and LaViolette, Alyce. *It Could Happen To Anyone: Why Battered Women Stay*, Sage Publications, Newbury Park, CA., 1993.

Blume, Sue. *Secret Survivors*, Ballantine Books, New York, N.Y., 1985.

Borysenko, Joan. *Guilt is the Teacher, Love is the Lesson,* Warner Books, New York, N.Y., 1990.

____. *Minding The Body, Mending The Mind*, Bantam Books, New York, N.Y., 1987.

Boumil, Marcia; Friedman, Joel; and Barbara Taylor. *Date Rape*, Health Communications, Inc., Deerfield Beach, FL., 1992.

277

Braswell, Linda. *Quest For Respect*, Pathfinder Publishing of California, Ventura, CA., 1989.

Briere, John N. *Child Abuse Trauma*, Sage Publications, Newbury Park, CA., 1992.

Brownmiller, Susan. *Against Our Will*, Fawcett Columbine, New York, N.Y., 1975.

Carlton, Jean. *Panic No More*, Stonehorse Press, Tulsa, OK., 1994.

Clift, Jean Dalby and Clift, Wallace B. *The Hero Journey In Dreams*, The Crossroad Publishing Co., New York, N. Y., 1991.

Davis, Flora. *Moving The Mountain*, Simon and Schuster, New York, N.Y., 1991.

Douglas, Claire. *The Woman In The Mirror*, Sigo Press, Boston, MA., 1990.

Ellis, Albert. *Anger: How To Live With And Without It*, Citadel Press, New York, N.Y., 1977.

Engel, Beverly. *The Emotionally Abused Woman*, Ballantine Books, New York, N.Y., 1990.

Faludi, Susan. *Backlash*, Anchor Books, New York, N.Y., 1991.

Fedders, Charlotte. *Shattered Dreams*, Dell Publishing, New York, N. Y. 1987.

Firestone, Robert. *The Fantasy Bond*, Human Sciences Press, Inc., New York, N.Y., 1987.

Figley, Charles. *Trauma and Its Wake*, Vol. 1, Brunner/Mazel Psychosocial Stress Series, New York, N.Y., 1985.

_____.*Trauma and Its Wake*, Vol. II, Brunner/Mazel Psychosocial Stress Series, New York, N.Y., 1986.

Forward, Susan; and Buck, Craig. *Betrayal of Innocence*, Penquin Books, New York, N.Y., 1978.

_____. *Men Who Hate Women And The Women Who Love Them*, Bantam Books, New York, N.Y., 1986.

____. *Obsessive Love*, Bantam Books, New York, N.Y., 1992.

____. *Toxic Parents*, Bantam Books, New York, N.Y., 1989.

Frankel, Lois. *Women, Anger & Depression*, Health Communications, Inc., Deerfield Beach, FL., 1992.

French, Marilyn. *The War Against Women*, Ballantine Books, New York, N.Y., 1992.

Gutek, Barbara A. *Sex And The Workplace*, Jossey-Bass Publishers, 1985.

Harary, Keith; Weintraub, Pamela. *Lucid Dreams in 30 Days*, St. Martin's Press, New York, N.Y., 1989.

Herman, Judith Lewis, *Trauma and Recovery*, Basic Books, New York, N.Y., 1992.

____. *Father-Daughter Incest*, Harvard University Press, Cambridge, MA., 1981.

Jung, Carl G. *Man And His Symbols*, Doubleday Windfall, New York, N.Y., 1964.

Kalmuss, D.S. "The Intergenerational Transmission of Marital Aggression," *Journal of Marriage and the Family, 46*, 11-19, 1984.

Kaufmann, Walter. *The Portable Nietzsche*, Viking Press, New York, N.Y. 1954, 1968.

Kirschner, Sam; Kirschner, Diana; and Rappaport, Richard. *Working With Adult Incest Survivors*, Brunner/Mazel, New York, N.Y., 1993.

Kluft, Richard. *Incest Related Syndromes of Adult Psychopathology*, American Psychiatric Press, Inc., Washington, D.C., 1990.

Knox, David. *Choices in Relationships: An Introduction to Marriage and the Family.* West Publishing Company, St. Paul, MN., 1991.

Kroll, Jerome. *PTSD/Borderlines In Therapy*, Norton, New York, N.Y., 1993.

Ledray, Linda. *Recovering From Rape*, Henry Holt and Co., New York, N.Y., 1986, 1994.

Leonard, Linda. *Meeting The Madwoman*, Bantam Books, New York, N.Y. 1993.

Lew, Mike. *Victims No Longer*, HarperCollings, New York, N.Y., 1988.

Manntooth, Carol; Geffner, Robert; Franks, Dawn; and Patrick, John. *Family Preservation: A Treatment Manual For Reducing Couple Violence,* Family Violence & Sexual Assault Institute, Tyler, Texas, 1987.

Matton, Mary Ann. *Understanding Dreams*, Spring Publications, Inc., Dallas, TX., Revised Edition, 1984.

McEvoy, Alan; and Brookings, Jeff. *If She Is Raped*, Learning Publications, Inc. Holmes Beach, FL., 1991, 1994.

McFarland, Barbara; and Baker-Baumann, Tyeis. *Feeding The Empty Heart*, Harper and Row, New York, N.Y., 1988.

Mellody, Pia; Miller, Andrea; and Miller, Keith. *Facing Love Addiction*, HarperSan Francisco, New York, N.Y., 1992.

Mendelsohn, Robert. *Male Practice, How Doctors Manipulate Women*, Contemporary Books, Inc., Chicago, IL., 1982.

Miller, Alice. *Banished Knowledge*, Doubleday, New York, N.Y., 1990.

_____. *Breaking Down The Wall Of Silence*, Meridian, New York, N.Y., 1991.

_____. *The Drama Of The Gifted Child,* Basic Books, New York, N.Y., Revised Edition,1994.

_____. *Thou Shalt Not Be Aware: Society's Betrayal Of The Child*, A Meridian Book, New York, N.Y., 1984.

Minirth, Frank; Meier, Paul; Hemfelt, Robert; Sneed, Sharon; & Hawkins, Don. *Love Hunger*, Ballantine, New York, N.Y.,1990.

Moore, Thomas. *Care Of The Soul*, HarperPerennial, New York, N.Y., 1992.

NiCarthy, Ginny. *Getting Free*, The Seal Press, Seattle, WA., 1982, 1986.

Putnam, Frank. *Diagnosis and Treatment of Multiple Personality Disorder*, The Guilford Press, New York, N.Y., 1989.

Roman, Sanaya. *Personal Power Through Awareness*, H. J. Kramer, Inc., Tiburon, CA., 1986.

Rosellini, Gayle; and Worden, Mark. *Of Course You're Angry*, HarperCollins Publishers, New York, N.Y., 1985.

Ross, Colin. *Multiple Personality Disorder*, Wiley-Interscience Publication, New York, N.Y., 1989.

Roth, Geneen. *When Food Is Love*, Penquin Books USA Inc., New York, N.Y., 1991.

Samuels, Michael. *Healing With The Mind's Eye*, Summit Books, New York, N.Y., 1990.

Sanford, John A. *Dreams and Healing*, Paulist Press, New York, N.Y., 1978.

Schaef, Anne Wilson. *Women's Reality*, Harper, New York, N.Y., 1981.

Schellenbaum, Peter. *The Wound Of The Unloved*, Element Books, Longmead, Shaftesbury, Dorset, England, 1988.

Sechrist, Elsie. *Dreams, Your Magic Mirror*, Dell Publishing Co., Inc., New York, N.Y., 1968.

Shuman, Sandra G. *Source Imagery*, Doubleday, New York, N.Y., 1989.

Slaby, Andrew. *After-Shock*, Villard Books, New York, N.Y., 1989.

Statman, Jan Berliner. *The Battered Woman's Survival Guide*, Taylor Publishing, Dallas, TX., 1990.

Steinem, Gloria. *Revolution From Within*, Little, Brown and Company, Boston, MA., 1992, 1993.

Stone, Merlin. *When God Was A Woman*, Harcourt Brace Jovanovich, Publishers, New York, N.Y., 1976.

Sumrall, Amber; and Taylor, Dena. *Sexual Harassment: Women Speak Out*, The Crossing Press, Freedom, CA., 1992.

Thomas, James M. *The Seven Steps to Personal Power*, Health Communications, Inc. Deerfield Beach, FL., 1992.

Tart, Charles. *Waking Up*, Shambahala, Boston, MA., 1986.

Tarvis, Carol. *Anger, The Misunderstood Emotion*, Simon & Schuster, New York, N.Y., 1982, 1989.

Terr, Lenore. *Too Scared To Cry*, Harper and Row, New York, N.Y., 1990.

Utain, Marsha; and Oliver, Barbara. *Scream*, Health Communications, Inc., Deerfield Beach, Fl., 1989.

Walker, Barbara. *The Battered Woman*, Harper & Row, New York, N.Y., 1979.

____. *The Crone*, HarperSan Francisco, CA., 1988.

Wallerstein, Judith S; and Blakeslle, Sandra. *Second Chances*, Tichnor and Fields, New York, N.Y., 1989.

Webb, Susan. *Shock Waves*, Master Media, New York, N.Y., 1994.

____. *Step Forward: Sexual Harassment in the Workplace*, Master Media, New York, N.Y., 1992.

Wolf, Naomi. *The Beauty Myth*, Anchor Books, New York, N.Y., 1991.

Zukav, Gary. *The Seat Of The Soul*, Simon & Schuster, New York, N.Y., 1989.

Index

VICTIM NO MORE

ORDER FORM

Telephone orders: (918) 488-9530

Postal Orders: Stonehorse Press
                        P.O. Box 701595
                        Tulsa, Oklahoma 74170

Please send me ___ copies of *Victim No More* @ $13.95 each.
Please send me ___ copies of *Panic No More* @ $12.95 each.

Name _____

Address _____

City _____ State _____ Zip _____

Telephone, including area code (_____)_____

Please include $1.24 for surface shipping.

Payment method:

____ Check _____ Visa _____ MasterCard

Card number _____ Exp. date: ___/___

Name on card _____

Thank you for your order.
Please call or write concerning bulk orders.